ONE PRESIDENT

Sam J. Cutrufelli Sr.

Gotham Books

30 N Gould St.
Ste. 20820, Sheridan, WY 82801
https://gothambooksinc.com/

Phone: 1 (307) 464-7800

© 2024 *Sam J. Cutrufelli Sr*. All rights reserved.

No part of this book may be reproduced, stored in a retrieval system, or transmitted by any means without the written permission of the author.

Published by Gotham Books (November 21, 2024)

ISBN: 979-8-3305-8383-6 (P)
ISBN: 979-8-3305-8384-3 (E)

Because of the dynamic nature of the Internet, any web addresses or links contained in this book may have changed since publication and may no longer be valid.

The views expressed in this work are solely those of the author and do not necessarily reflect the views of the publisher, and the publisher hereby disclaims any responsibility for them.

The world is getting smaller what was geographical is now international.

Can you handle it Mr. or Mrs. President?

Rolling along, rolling along, the train keeps rolling relentlessly towards its destination the Washington, D.C. train depot. I am on the train and my name is Donald Goldwater. I am a newspaper reporter and my destination is also Washington, D.C. My present assignment is to follow and report back to my father the last legs of the current presidential election. First a little about myself. I am twenty-seven years old; I have been raised in a newspaper family. My father is Isaac Goldwater and his longtime partner is Carl Steinberg. They were two of the most famous and admired journalists of their time. The two covered coronations of Kings and Queens. World War II both in and on the Atlantic side and the Pacific side, the Hindenburg flight from the United States across the Atlantic Ocean to Paris, France. The Lindberg child kidnapping and the birth of Israel, the baseball world series, plus every presidential contest. That was just to mention a few of their assignments.

When my father and Carl retired from active reporting, it was a big emotional letdown for them, so my father bought an active newspaper plant in Fremont, Vermont. His reason was "To keep my fingers in the pie". At the age of five, I was already an ink stained news hound. My father was the editor. My older sister Sally was for all practical purposes the chief. Sally ran the plant. My mother was not a bit interested in the affairs of the journalists. My mother was a landscape painter. She painted the sea, the boats wherever she could set-up her easel she was content. I worked at the paper part-time until I finished high school. After graduating I then went to Milwaukee, Wisconsin to get my degree in Journalism. The University had a full-fledged newspaper plant that rivaled some of the best commercial plants in the United States. I applied for a job as an assistant editor at the school. The president of the University knew of my father and Carl, so I was hired, sight unseen. The paper never had a professional editor. The University's president was the editor, but he had so many other tasks that being editor was just a title. The grunt work was done by myself, assistant editor. After two years as assistant, I was promoted to Editor.

I served as an editor until I graduated. After graduating, I drove back home to Vermont. I was to continue my journalistic journey with my father and sister. The paper had a part time reporter and an apprentice reporter. I was the full-time reporter for the paper. Like most small-time operations, I had to cover cats stranded in trees, the occasional burglary, city fires, and political meetings, P.T.A. functions anything and everything associated with news.

One day, my father came to me and said that I was ready for the big time as was the newspaper itself. He, my father wanted me to go to Washington, D.C. and cover the last leg of the current presidential contest. My father handed me a pocketful of cash plus a large manila envelope. The envelop contained photos and a brief summary of each remaining contestant and their chances of success. It happened quickly. He said "here is our ticket and "good-bye and good luck" and I was on my way. Scared but confident. The porter working my side of the train was a distinguished old train hand by the name of Wilbur. Wilbur was reared in the train business as I was in the news business. Wilbur's father was the head porter, and trained now, he had a desk at headquarters in Maine. Wilbur's wife was the head cook and she could cook, her name was Arlene and she made me a lamb sandwich that was the best ever. Wilbur and I hit it off from the start and he set me up a small office where I could layout my photos and study my dad's briefings and his personal opinion of each person's chances for success. The train finally reached the depot at Washington, D.C. I said my goodbyes to Wilbur and Arlene and disembarked. I hailed down a cab and gave the cabbie the address of Carl Steinberg.

    The cabbie waved off my offered address as he knew where Carl lived. Everyone in Washington D.C. knew where Carl lived. So, we took off and then finally we pulled up to a gated entrance that was Carl's estate. The driver got out of the taxi and went to a phone, fastened to a wall of the small shed used by an attendant when the gates were physically or I should say officially maned. Otherwise a person had to use the phone to make contact with the residence. Mildred answered the phone and the driver told Mildred of my arrival. I found out later that she was Carl's everything. Mildred was just that. Cook, boss lady of the estate, business manager. Mildred did it all and very efficiently. The cabbie and Mildred talked a minute and the cabbie laughed and said to not forget his white bag. The conversation was very cryptic, as all I could discern was the cabbie's conversation. He the cab driver did repeat the fact that Jeremiah would be arriving to pick me up and also bring this white bag. After the cabbie hung up he went to sit in the cab and wait for Jeremiah. I asked the driver "How much do I owe him?" He laughed and said "Thanks but no thanks, we cabbies don't charge to bring guests to Carl's place." Again, I was to find out that Carl, as was his father were the city's largest philanthropist. They contributed to schools, churches and about every social function in Washington, D.C. The cab driver could not say enough about the Steinberg's kindness to the city and its people. If Jeremiah did not arrive when he did, I guess he would still be talking. I mean the cab driver.

Jeremiah arrived he was about the biggest man I had ever seen. How about that he was six feet seven or eight or taller, and about three-hundred and fifty pounds of solid muscle, no fat. Boy was he huge. He never said a word he just nodded to the driver and myself. He then handed the cab driver the mysterious white bag. The cab driver said "Yum" and drove off. I was beginning to wonder about the folks of D.C. Jeremiah loaded my three bags in an overextended golf cart. I got inside the cart and he drove to the entrance that was Carl's mansion. I was almost floored when Jeremiah spoke his first words. He said "My name is Jeremiah and I oversee the grounds and fix up around here." "I'll drive you to where you will be living while you are Carl's guest". Jeremiah drove about three blocks from the main house and pulled up to a guest house of which there was a total of three all alike.

Each guest house had a two-car garage. Jeremiah pressed the remote he had, and the garage door opened. Inside was a Chevy Taurus. A golf cart similar to what we were driving, a motor scooter and three bicycles. He opened the front door to the cottage and bought my three bags inside the door. He said "Mildred will call me later" he then proceeded to hand me the keys to the cottage. He said for me to use the car and handed me the keys. Then he disappeared. I was left alone and a little confused. Presently, Mildred called and said for me to drive over as she was anxious to meet me. Mildred apologized for Carl not being present to greet me, but he would see Carl at dinner which was to be at seven p.m. that evening. We hung up the phone and I drove to the main house.

I parked in a designated parking spot and walked up the stairs to the front door and rang the bell and waited very apprehensively. The door opened and I was bear hugged by a gorgeous woman big in stature. Between hugs she mentioned that she was Mildred. What a woman Mildred was all of six foot three, light complexion in color but had predominately some sort of island heritage. Mildred was all of three hundred pounds. Mildred said for me to come in. I was escorted to a large garden room that overlooked a vast manicured lawn interspersed with flowers of many types. Mildred excused herself as she said she would get some coffee and cookies. Mildred arrived with a cart loaded with coffee, cakes and cookies. Mildred poured coffee and we had cookies than she said that all the cab drivers got white bags of chocolate chip cookies. Some of the cab drivers would bring a fare to the house and tell Mildred that they were sightseeing when in reality they came for the chocolate chip cookies.

We drank coffee and ate cookies than Mildred opened up and she talked about my dad and Carl. Mildred had a hilarious story about Jeremiah who I just learned was Mildred's husband. Here is the story as told to me between sips of coffee and of course chocolate chip cookies. Jeremiah graduated from college as an honor student majoring in mathematics. After his graduation, Jeremiah had a very hard time finding employment in his field. He was literally unemployed for over one year. He lived on low level jobs just to exist. Jeremiah finally got a break. It was not exactly what he wanted but it was a teaching job at a small private academy. It was teaching math, his major. It wasn't a high-level university, but it was a step forward. He was at his job for about a year when he had a severe setback. He was diagnosed with a brain clot, which left him with incoherent speech and memory loss. Jeremiah had to have immediate hospital care. He advised his superiors' and was given a leave of absence. He had to have immediate surgery and the surgery was a success. The convalescence was to be at least three to six months. He finally got back to work, but things were never the same. He had to wear a turban until his surgery was completely healed. That with his enormous stature and also being the only teacher of color in an all-white school gave some of the students a false anxiety.

A meeting was held and most of the parents wanted Jeremiah dismissed. The faculty was forced to dismiss Jeremiah with the excuse that the math program was going to be combined with a science program and so the math position would be non-existent. Jeremiah was now unemployed again. This go around him was luckier. He was having lunch and at the table was a professor Howard Hughes. The two struck up a conversation, small world that it sometimes is, and it was revealed that Howard Hughes was the principal of a prestigious school and by chance he needed a math teacher. Coincidence sometimes proved to be opportunities unexpected and unexplainable, but they do exist. Jeremiah was to be employed as a part time math teacher. It so happened that the existing math teacher was an Army Major, Major Jurgins. The army was in need of a math teacher and Major Jurgins was to report to camp for active duty. His papers said to report at eight am on June 30th, which was exactly five days from now. Jeremiah was to come to the school tomorrow and he and the professor would meet with Major Jurgins to discuss the capacity of the position.

Major Jurgins said he did not know how long he would be gone. The army had no definite time for his use it could be three months, one year or forever. Jeremiah and the professor chatted, while they waited for Major Jurgins to be free from his class, then he would be free to meet with Jeremiah and the professor. Major Jurgins was standing outside his classroom and he looked down the hall and he saw Jeremiah and the professor walking side by side towards him when he burst out laughing. It was contagious for Jeremiah and the professor also burst out laughing but they had no clue as to why. Finally, it came to light between burst of laughter that the Major explained that he was seeing the most extraordinary vision his eyes had ever seen, walking down the hall was the professor who was a slight five-foot-tall and big around as a ball, besides him was this tall turbaned colored giant, six foot eight, three-hundred and fifty pound, it was too much for the normal eyes to perceive. So, he started laughing again as did Jeremiah and the professor.

The professor was the first to stop laughing and said that we should get on with our meeting. When the Major calmed down he pointed a finger at Jeremiah and said "Who might you be?" Jeremiah answered in his best southern voice; I be "Jeremiah" from Mississippi. That brought on another bout of laughter. The laughing ended when Miss O'Malley the vice principal poked her head in the room and said you children calm down your disturbing the classes. So, the fun ended. The professor than formally introduced Jeremiah Hanks to Major Jergins and left the room. Major Jergins briefed Jeremiah as to his responsibilities and they said their goodbyes. The major would be leaving over the weekend, as it was the job lasted for over a year and it was the best work Jeremiah ever had. The Major informed professor Hughes that his army time was over and that he would be back a week from now. Jeremiah again looked for employment, but work was scarce.

Professor Hughes was retiring from his position and Miss O'Malley was to succeed him. Jeremiah went to see Professor Hughes and thanked him for the best job he ever had. The professor was very glad to see his friend again, but they concluded that they could not solve all the world's problems, the professor asked Jeremiah if he would be partial to doing other than teaching jobs if was available, though it might be a lessor job. The two left on friendly terms and Jeremiah assured the professor that a lessor job would not hurt his ego. Two days later, professor Hughes telephoned Jeremiah and said that he talked to a good friend of a Carl Steinberg and that Carl needed a grounds superintendent and Jeremiah needed employment. Jeremiah got the position. It was to be the most fruitful day of his life as he met me. She, Mildred, got tears in her eyes and excused herself. When she reappeared, she said Jeremiah and her fell in love and she became Mrs. Mildred Hanks. God bless Carl and Professor Hughes for bringing such happiness to my life. The meeting was over, but we continued eating chocolate chip cookies and drinking coffee. As I left Mildred reminded me that dinner would be at seven o'clock. I left Mildred and drove back to the guest house.

Jeremiah and his crew were in the midst of sprucing up the grounds of the three guest cottages. Guest houses they were but not the average guest houses. Each home was situated on a two-and-a-half-acre plot that was beautifully landscaped. There were hundreds of pits of foreign plants interspecies throughout the acreage in and among different varieties of low growing ivy. The pathways were made up of which rock with a redwood border. The paths led from the back of the house and rambled throughout the property. Every so often a beautiful pruned tree would be seen to accent the natural look. Magnolias of different species were abundant. Bricks were also carefully grouped throughout. Along the fence line there were many vines plus many Italian cypress trees that stood tall and majestic. They formed a beautiful green screen of foliage that separated the three guest houses. Jeremiah pointed out that each sitting area. The sitting areas were framed with white rock and paths led to each area. Each sitting area had its own gazebo surrounded by assorted tables and chairs that blended in with the natural look of nature. There was no glitz or chrome prevalent with so many modern contrivances. The look was to be natural and so it was. Thanks to Carl, we the guest experienced living in the City, but also living with nature and all her glory.

I left Jeremiah and his crew and went to the guest house to finish unpacking and rest some before dinner. So far it was an exhilarating experience. I came to D.C. as a journalist and learned that in life we can have our cake and eat it. I arrived at the mansion at the appointed time for dinner and rang the bell and was surprised to be greeted by Jeremiah. Jeremiah ushered me into the dining room. Carl was in a wheelchair and was seated at the head of an enormous table. The table was covered with goodies. I was seated next to Carl. I remembered when I was a kid, Carl was a dashing journalist. To see him now was sad as the now Carl was a mere resemblance of what I remembered. We greeted each other and he was generally happy to see the son of his former journalist partner, my dad. Naturally he talked and asked about my father. He said my father was the most prolific journalist of their era. He asked about my mother who he said was my father's backbone. He asked about my sister and said she always had printers ink smudges on her hands and face and clothing. Carl said if you were in newspaper you had ink on you no doubt about it. Then Mildred came into the room and made everyone welcomed. Carl and I exchanged little remembrances of the past throughout the meal. Carl said it was past his bedtime, so we adjourned early. Carl and I agreed to meet tomorrow and talk about the going presidential election which was the main reason that I was in D.C. I was apprehensive and restless all night. Carl was by far the most authorative person to discuss the election with although he was wheelchair bound, somehow, he knew by far more than most what to expect.

Tomorrow could not come soon enough. Mildred walked me to the door and we talked a few moments about Carl's health and the wonderful dinner. She reminded me that I was family not only a guest. And that I was to have lunch and dinner with the family. Breakfast was another thing. If you were in the house you were welcome to a European style breakfast of coffee confection fruit, toast. Mildred said breakfast was on the go. Jeremiah started work at six-thirty a.m. and he usually had toast and coffee with Mildred. Carl had breakfast in his room. So, it would be just Mildred and I. Carl's routine was breakfast, then at ten a.m. each day he had appointments until lunch. He then devoted the rest of the day to himself. Mildred said Carl could meet with me at one p.m. I said it would be fine and left for my cottage.

The next morning, I called Mildred and told her that I would be coming for breakfast. She gave me a large bag of goodies. Being a bachelor, I was adept at making coffee and with the cookies I splurged. I told Mildred that I would be at the house around eleven a.m. after cookies and coffee. I went to the gazebo there and I had more coffee and cookies as I scanned the notes my father gave me. It was cookies, coffee and notes not necessarily in that order. It was heaven on earth. Mildred, Jeremiah and I had a light lunch and I was taken to Carl's library. Another shock was how many could I survive? The room was gigantic with fifteen-foot ceilings and every inch of wall space was covered with shelves and books, books and books. Rolling ladders were attached to the ceilings to get books up high. Even with the ladders how in the world could a wheelchair ridden person get a book from ten to fifteen feet in the air? I would learn the answer to that question later, but it was nevertheless intriguing. For the time being, all I could do was to be prepared for another shock at any given moment.

Carl was at a huge mahogany table and at his side were a couple of trolleys filled with books and reference material. Carl and I greeted each other, and Mildred excused herself and left. There I was along with the man in his environment and I was speechless. In order to compose myself and not appear as a complete idiot I blurted out that Mildred was quite an extraordinary woman that seemed to break the ice. Carl said "Donald I know you came here this afternoon to debate and talk about the candidates but they can wait a bit while I tell you a little about Mildred." Where to begin, I guess it would be with my father and Mildred's mother. Yes, that's where it began. Susan was her name and she came to work for my father in the same capacity that Mildred is now. Susan's husband was a low life and he was completely joked on drugs and alcohol. The only good thing he ever did in his life was to die early and give peace to Susan and her daughter, Mildred. He died of liver problems.

Susan met her husband right here on the grounds. He worked for my father as a handyman. When sober, he was good but for all practical purposes but he was a failure and a waste. My father let the family live in the servant's quarters. Keyjo was his name. He was missing for about three days when they discovered his body in a remote area of the property. He was apparently on a binge that ended his life. Whenever he went on his binges, he would go to this area where he had a crude shack. So Susan and Mildred were now alone. Mildred attended school and helped her mother with the chores after school. One day as she was walking to school, she passed the athletic field where the track team was practicing for a meet. Mildred was intrigued with the exercising and practicing going on. Two girls were watching what was going on also. Mildred knew one of the girls who upon seeing Mildred called out to her to come and meet the other girl. There was a shotput pit close by with three boys heaving the heavy ball. One of the boys spotted the three girls and came over to them. He asked Mildred if she ever participated in sports. Mildred replied "No", but that she was interested. At that time Mildred was already a big in size girl. She asked the boy if she could feel the weight of the ball. The guy gave her the shotput ball and gave her some rudimentary lessons and told her to give the ball a toss. To everyone's surprise she tossed the ball almost as far as the school's number one shot putter. About that time, the track coach appeared and asked what was going on. He gave Mildred her lesson and told the coach a star was born. Of course, he was being a smarty pants but the coach was not amused. The coach talked to Mildred an asked her if she would like to try out and make the team. Unfortunately, the girls track team did not have a field program which would include shot putting, javelin and pole vaulting. The coach said that they were entertaining options to include the field events for the girl's team, but nothing significant has been reached. For the interim period she could try out with the boys. If she made the team, history would be made as no girl ever competed with the boys. If Mildred agreed to try out for the team, she would be facing many obstacles. First and foremost were her chores at the mansion, she could not let her mother down. Secondary her homework and schooling had to fit in. For a fourteen-year-old girl it was a lot to ask for. Before the coach parted, he asked Mildred if she would mind throwing a few shots. She tossed the ball about four times and the coach was amazed. She truly could be a star in the making.

Carl stopped talking for a few minutes as he had to address Mildred who came into the library. Mildred was accompanied with a teenage boy. The three talked for a few minutes and then Mildred was left alone. The boy apparently knew the routine as he started putting books on the shelves. Carl took another few minutes to enlighten me as to what was going on. Carl said that each day at about this time a school aged child would come to the library. The child would be paid to assist Carl in placing the books that Carl used for his research back in their place on the shelves. That explained the question in my mind as to how Carl managed to get his books from the shelves. Carl again resumed his narrative about young Mildred. Mildred was able to solve her problems and she made the track team. Needless to say, she excelled in the shot put. She was so good that she beat out all the boys and she became the number one shot putter on the team. She was so good that in her first year she earned a spot in the state track finals. This was amazing to try out for the state finals in her first year.

Mildred was now fifteen years old and she finished third in the finals, competing against boys that were in the sport for three or four seasons. Mildred was a phenomenal athlete as a girl. The second year of track and academics were good and bad. The good was that her team won every track meet and she was the star. Scholastically she managed to keep up her schooling with straight A's and B's plus, handle doing her chores. What a load for a young girl, the bad was that her mother died of an illness that was not expectant. Mildred was fifteen years old going on one hundred and how she endured it all was too much to comprehend. Shortly thereafter, Carl's father passed away. Carl had to take a leave of absence from his journalistic work. The estate had many business and personal problems that had to be attended to. Carl's father was involved in many political groups, plus he was the single highest philanthropist in the City of D.C. I came home to an unbelievable amount of problems. Believe it or not if fifteen years old Mildred was not there I probably would have been totally overwhelmed although I had lawyers and advisors galore. Thank God for her. She became the best track and field girl that the city of D.C. ever had. Sadly, she had to give all that up now to run the estate.

Mildred had to leave school and attend night school so she could get her diploma. It was a rough ride for her and me. Donald, before we get on with our political work there is a little more of Mildred, you opened a can of worms when you said Mildred was exceptional. One day, Mildred and a girlfriend were doing some errands. One of the errands was to take some lunch to the girl's brother. The brother was training to be a boxer at the local gym. The gym had both professional and amateurs doing their routines. The brother took the sister and Mildred for a tour of the gym and to introduce them to the trainees. In one corner of the gym there was one girl wrestler in the ring and she was introduced to Mildred and friend. She was touted as the best wrestler in that club and quite possibly all of D.C. The girl was not very friendly and she was pouting over the fact that her wrestling partner stood her up and so she was not training. Her routine was messed up. She was training for a bout so she needed the workout. The woman wrestler looked down at Mildred and said "Hey big girl" want to wrestle with me or are you afraid to get squashed. The girl threw a few more unfriendly taunting at Mildred, but Mildred said she had errands to do but would wrestle with her some other time. That set the girl up to being absolutely furious, she said Mildred was frightened to face her. Mildred had had enough. She asked her friend if she could find her some gym clothes. They went into the girl's locker room and found some clothes for Mildred to wear. The whole gym stopped training as word got about that a wrestling exhibition was to take place. So, they all got around the ring to watch Mildred get slaughtered. The girl wrestler was now in her element and she said Mildred was so scarred that she probably left via the back door. But to everyone's surprise Mildred came over to the ring. There was an ex pug that trained some of the boys and he said he would referee. So, the bout began as was expected and the girl wrestler was good, very good but Mildred held her own due to her natural athletics' physical ability. The girl wrestler knew she had truly got herself into something she never dreamed about. After a few rounds the girl wrestler said she had enough, and she had other schedules to attend to. She was a champ and she praised Mildred and told everyone that Mildred was as good as anyone she had ever faced. The girl tried to sign Mildred up, but Mildred said her plate was full. The girl wrestler was not giving up so easily she told Mildred that she could make her a champ. Mildred held her ground and said that it was impossible at this time. The two girls left the gym to finish their errands. Mildred's friend said that her brother said they still talk about the event to this day. End of story now Donald let's get on to our political appraisals.

So, I opened the folder that my father gave me. Inside were the hopefuls and the challenges for the president of the U.S. There were sixteen eight by ten glossy prints of each person plus a short biography of each as to what they were and what they are. Carl laid out all the prints on the table and in his methodical way would pick up a glossy photograph and examine it from all angles. Then he would set it down and read what father said of the person. "Ah" he would say Mrs. Friday Darlington good girl, good girl. Former Governor of Michigan. Then he would pick up another and another. With each one he would make a comment. Carl was getting tired, so he begged off and he assured me that tomorrow there would be no distractions. My father holds me that Carl had so much knowledge about almost everything that it was almost impossible for him to approach any subject without adding an antidote or two or three. Carl said more diversions. Yeah, we will see.

The following morning, I went into D.C. to take in some firsthand political gossip. My press card was examined and there I was among my peers. Conceivably it was a scene similar to what Carl and my father went through each election year. In the press room the walls were covered with photographs of all the runners from both parties. It was still early on in the race. Still twelve months to go, but already some were saying this one would win or that one had no change. Carl would probably say "We'll see my boy, yes, we will." Carl's not a pessimist but he has seen front runners today and has been tomorrow. So, I mostly listened, drank coffee and smoked too much. All in all, it was a good trip. Occasional one of the contestants would come to the press room and spout glitzy galore why he or she would be the next president. I arrived back at the estate in time for lunch in his room. Carl's and my meeting were not cancelled but put on hold. As it turned out Carl was feeling better and he informed Mildred that he would meet with me in the library at two p.m. After lunch I freshened up a bit and anxiously waited for father time to the library. Carl was already there. He did not waste anytime apparently today was going to be all business. Carl examined all the photos again as he did and he would say "no chance to one and lay it aside." Then another was a longshot. He finally had four too choose from the others had very little change so Carl thought. It took a whole bunch of dollars and many influential people and money corporations to be a front runner. Debates, gossip, experience were all going to enter into the picture. Carl said it would be one of these four. Two republications and two democrats were laid out for me. Four targets for today. Carl and my father both actually believed that if Mr. Bizzar had entered into the arena, he was so huge that anything could happen. Point to tell a few years back, a few elections back entered Judge Samuel Stein. Judge Stein was the senior Judge of Wyoming for twenty years. Judge Stein was regarded by the Wyoming Democrats party and also the nations democratic party as the best choice for Governor of Wyoming if he elected to run for that office. He had twenty years of experience. Judge Stein was regarded by the Wyoming Democratic Party as the best choice for Governor of Wyoming if he elected to run for that office. Judge Stein was very well in liking and he had no scandals and he had a good marriage. His father Isaac Stein was probably the most powerful figure in the state of Wyoming. He was the most powerful Democrat. He was by far the wealthiest person in Wyoming. Mr. Isaac Stein owned the largest sheep business in Wyoming. Acres and acres of land to accommodate his sheep enterprise. He was the largest donator to the Democratic Party. His largest was evident as he contributed to building of schools, parks, churches. None of Mr. Senior Stein's virtues would hurt his son. The existing Governor was stepping down, he cited that his existing health problems would hurt the state of Wyoming. He then committed himself to backing Judge Stein if the Judge decided to run. This endorsement would not hurt the Judge as the present Governor was well liked and admired.

The Judge announces his candidacy for the Governor of Wyoming. The reason he held back to run was so that the other candidates could blast each other and eventually narrow the field. Two weeks into his campaign. Mr. Big Bizzar entered the picture and the election was never the same. Judge Stein and his wife were not the compatible couple that the public was meant to see. Mrs. Stein actually hated her husband, the Judge, and also her father in law. Isaac Stein. Why? Mrs. Stein said that Isaac Stein belittled her many times claiming that his son married beneath himself, also she had a thing about the property that she and her husband shared here is how that went. Isaac Stein was an exceedingly successful corporate lawyer. He decided to sell his huge firm and retire, which he did. The firm that bought his law firm wanted Isaac Stein to remain on the board as an advisor, but Isaac Stein said he was retiring and retired he did. When Isaac was not doing legal work, he was looking for properties. He loved to buy land, Mr. Stein purchased two separate pieces of property that were attached to each other.

The front piece was 150 acres it was developed to the extent that it had a seven thousand square foot, two story colonial home with entrance columns. There was also a five-stall horse barn, a guest cottage, assorted barns and a large implement building for the farm equipment. Mr. Stein envisioned living there upon his retirement. The back property as he called it was one hundred twenty-five acres of underdeveloped land. It was land locked and joined the front acreage at the rear of the front acreage. The two parcels were neglected. When the original owners died the heirs had no interest in the property so it was put up for sale.

The economy was in a slump and it lasted for years. The property each unsold. Isaac Stein was able to buy the two parcels below the market value so it was an exceptional acquisition. Now comes the reason for Mrs. Stein's problem with the property. Samuel Stein and his finance were engaged for a long time, but the plan was to get married at some period. Elder Mr. Stein foresaw legitimate or imagined flaws in the son's relationship. Being a successful lawyer, his training was to always try to eliminate any and all loop holes regarding any document or legal matter. Mr. Stein figured that his son Samuel would eventually marry so he decided to legally split off a twenty-five-acre parcel from the front acreage. He then had a few thousand square foot house plus a modest guest house built on the property. For all intents and purposes the property was young Samuel Stein's residence. Now elder Isaac Stein leased the property when his son married, and the now Mrs. Stein assumed it was a marriage gift. Isaac Stein was protecting his and his son's best interest, but that was the mentality that made him an exceptional lawyer. The divorce was the social event of the year. Mrs. Stein's lawyers filed the divorce papers due to incompatibility and the messy go around began. Judge Stein and his aspirations of being elected Governor of Wyoming were going to be tested as never before. That's what I mean when bizarre events happen. From being bizarre events happen. From being a shoo in to a maybe, takes its toll. Mrs. Stein hired good lawyer's in fact very good lawyers. They were able to make some inroads, but Judge Stein proved to be clean. He did not go out drinking. He was not a womanizer. Judge Stein was a rock that had to be chiseled down. The lawyers told Mrs. Stein they needed a blockbuster. Mrs. Stein was relentless; she did not like to lose. With the aid of bazar happenings, they found what they thought would break the ice. It's a long story but it has to be told, so here we go.

When Isaac Stein sold his lawyer firm, he was like many retirees, but he also had more options. He was wealthy, in fairly good shape for his age and furthermore restless. Mrs. Stein decided to sell his home in Cheyenne and move into the colonial house on his acreage. It was a good move but also a more strife with problems. The old colonial had to be completely remodeled. The outlying buildings had to be worked on. Access had to be built to have legal access to the rear parcel. He also had to take trips to Australia where he had three properties. Quite an undertaking for a not too young man. One thing he soon found out was he had to think more and work less. So, with that in mind he had to have a game plan. So, his nimble mind began working, what would it take to make the land workable and profitable. He thought of farming, but he thought that would be like putting your head in a lion's mouth. He thought of cattle ranching, but he figures he needed much more land. It was an option. Sometimes you can't see what's right in front of you.

Sheep, Australia was sheep country. Sheep all over the place that was it, he would be a Wyoming sheep rancher. So, he lived sheep, studied sheep shearing, sheep contests and sheep school. He made appointments with prominent sheep ranchers and sheep wholesalers. Finally, he thought he was ready. One of the wholesalers met with him at the property now called Stein and Son Sheep Ranch. The make like the layout and suggested to start with two-hundred head also you need a good sheep hand. A Mr. Williams was the man. He had a large family and a hard-working wife. They knew sheep terms were agreed upon. The Williams moved into the guest house. Too small, no problem, the older boys, twelve, fourteen and sixteen slept in the barn. Two hundred sheep were trucked in. Four dogs that the Williams owner were brought in. They were trained sheep dogs. So, Stein and Son sheep ranch became a live working facility soon to become the largest sheep ranch in Wyoming and for part in the United States. The Williams involved with Stein were two brothers, Hugh Williams who came to the U.S. to manage Isaacs's ranch. Hughes brother Jerry was the elder and he owned and operated a small sheep ranch in Australia. Hugh worked for his brother, but the lack of money was a constant worry that his job might be in jeopardy. So, when Isaac hired Hugh, he took a big load off Hugh's shoulders.

The Stein and Son sheep ranch got off to a good start so that Isaac Stein was able to go to Australia and make some decisions regarding his three acreage there. Hugh contacted his brother and told him to expect Mr. Stein to advise him if necessary. Jerry Williams and Mr. Stein hit it off from the day they met. Jerry convinced Mr. Stein to turn his three parcels into a Stein and Son Sheep ranch of Australia. Jerry Stein sold his ranch to Mr. Stein and was hired to be the general manager. Jerry's small ranch was near his three parcels, so it was convenient to oversee all. Mr. Stein was going to use the same format that worked in Wyoming. That would be bringing in too hundred or three hundred head of sheep to the three parcels. The second Stein and son sheep ranch was on its way to shortly become Australia's number two, the De Vargas sheep ranch was the largest in Australia. There was the founder Elder De Vargas plus his three sons. When Mr. De Vargas retired, he put his youngest son to run the company. The younger son was very steady and was a wonderful family man. His middle son was Don De Vargas. Don was not married and liked the high life, partying and womanizing which ultimately was responsible for elder Mr. De Vargas to appoint the younger De Vargas to manage the company, although Don De Vargas was far the superior sheep person in all of Australia. To pacify his son, Mr. De Vargas decided to try to duplicate Isaac Stein's strategy. Mr. De Vargas had one big advantage he had a distant relative that was widowed and she and her husband had a good-sized ranch coincidently bordering on Isaac Stein's ranch. The window proposed to Mr. De Vargas to buy the two hundred and fifty-acre ranch that was up and running but at that time Mr. De Vargas was not interested. Now he was and a deal was made. Don De Vargas was to go to Wyoming and come to the United States. Don De Vargas and Judge Stein lives meshed regarding his divorce. When Don De Vargas arrived at his new home, he was not too pleased with the house the former owners lived in. He said it was a piece of junk. Nevertheless, he and his older brother moved in. The older brother was not a sheep man, he was an accountant and worked for a coal miner, coal mining industry was really in a slump. He was laid off with a large group follower. Meyer De Vargas was a divorced man he and his former wife has one child affected with autism. His former wife left Meyer and her son for parts unknown. Meyer needed work so his father put him in the office and he was to work for and with Don De Vargas in the States. Meyer was just the opposite of Don De Vargas he was very steady and did not drink or gamble or womanize. He was an exceptionally talented accountant, but he never had success with his own money, because he never made much. His ex-wife figured him a loser and she wanted better and more, hence the divorce. The new De Vargas ranch was not totally run down, but it needed a good leader and Don De Vargas was just the man. His love for the business superseded his other flaws. The ranch was such that it would that although it needed much improvement, yet it held its own as far as profit and loss. Already, Don De Vargas was meeting with architects and planners for his new home. When completed it would be a showpiece. Six months later he moved into his new home and the ex-owner's home was remodeled so that it was the hub of the ranch.

Offices were installed, a large conference room. Outside the graveled area was paved and tripped. All in all, the projection was some in and do business with me. The new Don De Vargas home was designed for entertaining. Inside and out. It had seven large bedrooms each with private baths. It had a twenty-four hundred square foot guest house that was not a detached unit but attached to the main house. The guest house had its own entrance and a three-car garage, but it also opened up into the main house. After the house and landscaping were completed. Don De Vargas was planning an open house. Two hundred invitations were sent out. Isaac and Samuel were to be guests of honor, so everyone was excited and anxious for the festivities to begin Don De Vargas was going to bring in a catered that knew barbecuing so they were going to barbecue whole pigs and of course lamb and prime rib roasts.

The gala event was a way of bringing together the top personalities and of course it all came down to the promoting the new found Wyoming sheep branch. Since Don De Vargas short time in America's he was a whirlwind of energy. Attending parties, meetings anything to promote his business had his attention. Isaac Stein frequently was seen at some of the same events, so Isaac Stein and Don De Vargas became friends although they would be fierce competitors. The open house would be the first time that the four most involved people in the trial of Judge Stein would be present the same time. They were Don De Vargas his brother Meyer De Vargas, Isaac Stein and of course Judge Stein.

They were careful to not discuss the trial, as the lawyers from both sides would pounce on any advantage that might ensue. Don De Vargas heard of Judge Stein moving out of his home so he asked the Judge where he was now living. Judge Stein said he was at his father's home temporarily but that was going to change as soon as possible. Don De Vargas said he would like to talk further to the Judge about his residency, but they did not think this was the appropriate time so he holds Isaac and his son that he would get in touch shortly and arrange for lunch. That settle they went about their business of back slapping and whatever happens at these events. Actually, the four people we spoke of the two De Vargas brothers at this time were not part of the litigation presented by Mrs. Stein's lawyers. But like I said if buzzer happening are in the making buzzer would make the most of it. A few days later Don De Vargas got in touch with Isaac and they set up a lunch meeting at Don De Vargas home. Isaac arrived punctually and were greeted affably by Don De

Vargas. Drinks were served and a wonderful lunch of petrol sole was satisfactorily consumed. After they had coffee and desert, Don De Vargas opened up the conversation with the fact that his newly built guest house would be available for the Judge for as long as he wanted to use it and he was to take meals with Don De Vargas at his liking. Both of the Isaac's were overwhelmed at the generous offer. Judge Stein accepted and details of when he would move in were discussed Isaac offered to pay Don De Vargas but Don De Vargas said he would be insulted if they continued taking payment. Judge Stein would be his guest period. The Judge had other options but this was by far the best considering the lawsuit. It was convenient to his father's home and he also had the convenience of using his office which was located on his property.

The office was attached to the Judge's guest house but was a separate identity. It was completely isolated do he did not need to infringe upon his home where Mrs. Stein was living and if guests were in the guest house, they would be immune to the Judges going and comings. The arrangement with Don De Vargas was perfect, as he would have complete privacy from Mrs. Stein's investigators and lawyers as the De Vargas private domain was completely enclosed with a beautiful six-foot wrought iron fence. To enter the grounds was by appointment only or certain people had remotes to operate gates and such. The convenience was especially welcomed when Judge Stein had to meet with his lawyers at the De Vargas guest house. Judge Stein and his father were not aware of how this move would come to haunt them I the near future, but for now it was ideal.

The statures regarding the Stein's divorce was ho hum some ups and some downs. Mrs. Stein told her lawyers they needed to find a blockbuster to assure victory. It seems that she read the script somewhere because accidently it seems that they might just have found one, it went like this, Mrs. Stein was a beautiful model at one time, she still is gorgeous. When her father and mother were killed in a boating accident, she being the only heir inherited the small but well maintained five-acre parcel and a nice two-story home. The mother and father gave their daughter all the advantages conceivable so the daughter could succeed. So, they had built an Olympic sized pool for the family although it was mainly for the daughter to keep her lovely shape intact. They also had a professional size tennis court on the property. These amenities were enjoyed by all members of the family as they were all fiendish about health and nutrition. Mrs. Stein also inherited considerable amount of stocks and money. She never sold the property but used it as a getaway after an exhausting modeling in say France or Italy wherever.

She married Judge Stein and resigned from modeling she moved to Cheyenne where her husband was based. Occasionally she would open the house and have a party or gathering. A good friend of the family had a daughter that was also a model and the daughter was getting married and her future husband owned the modeling agency that the daughter modeled for. It was headquartered in Paris, France so Mrs. Stein decided to alleviate some of her tensions due mainly because of her pending divorce and have a farewell party for the newlyweds who would be living in Paris. Mrs. Stein was very adept at throwing parties due to the circumstances of being in the public eye and the Judge's elections. Mrs. Stein sent out about one hundred invitations included were invited to Don De Vargas and his brother Jerry. It so happened that Don De Vargas could not attend due to previous scheduled obligations. Jerry was please to attend. Jerry and Mrs. Stein's mind was always working. She was aware that her husband was living at the guest house of the De Vargas. Also, that Jerry lived there. Jerry had a large cottage with a private bath and an adjourning small living area that had a television and stereo unit and assorted comfortable sofas and matching chairs. So, Mrs. Stein figures that she might get some details regarding her husband firsthand from Jerry, but she was so busy being the hostess that she could not play her bag of tricks on Jerry. So, she told or asked Jerry to stay over a day or so as she had plenty of spare bedrooms and a couple of other guests were also staying on but this was a play to get the rather shy Jerry alone. It worked. After the party was over, she showed Jerry to a bedroom that was nicely furnished and she kissed Jerry on the cheek and said for him to sleep well. She would have breakfast waiting for him. I wonder what went through Jerry's mind. Whatever scheme Mrs. Stein was working on was more than she bargained for. She called her head lawyer a told him to come see her immediately as she thought she found her blockbuster. Mrs. Stein inherited a substantial interest in the local golf club and its hotel so she was always catered to when she came home to visit, he called the manager of the club and arranged to have an office reserved for her and her attorney also they would be having breakfast. It was arranged for the next morning at nine a.m. After the two attorneys and she had breakfast they waited anxiously for Mrs. Stein to open up the business end of the meeting. During breakfast it was all social gossip i.e., world news and etc. Mrs. Stein said she would give a little background information. The De Vargas family was the largest ranching firm in Australia. The founder was the father plus he had three sons which formed the principals of the company.

The youngest De Vargas was a family man and dedicated to his father and the business. When the father retired the young son was made the head of the company. Don De Vargas was the middle child and he never married and was noted for his partying and womanizing. He was also very tuned into the business. In fact, he was the more logical choice to run the business, but his personal extravagances held him back. At the same time, elder Mr. De Vargas was entering a new market in Wyoming and made Don De Vargas the head of that second venture. The third son was the oldest and not a rancher he was an accountant so that gives you a little background of the family De Vargas. Why was this brought up, Mrs. Stein said that the De Vargas of America were going to be the central figures in her divorce. She went on. The new home Don De Vargas had built was like a fortress so Jerry De Vargas was their wooden horse to the property and Don De Vargas and my husband Judge Stein. So, when she had her party, she sent an invitation to Jerry De Vargas to attend. Her idea was to try to get some information regarding Samuel Stein as he was more or less free from the eyes of reporters and her own investigators being holed up in the Don De Vargas home.

She went on to tell that she extended her invitation for Jerry De Vargas to stay at her home as a guest. Also Mr. & Mrs. Everturn were staying on as guests. The guest rooms overlooked the landscaped property and the enormous pool. Each guest room had a small private deck accessible by a pair of French doors. This particular morning Mrs. Stein was enjoying the pool. She called out to Jerry to come and join her which he did. He asked about the Evers and Mrs. Stein said that they got an emergency call so they had to leave. As it was, she admitted to her lawyers there was no extended invitation to the Evers so she had told Jerry a little lie because she knew that Jerry was shy and she did not want to miss the opportunity. So, at breakfast she continued her fabrication but not before Jerry opened the door. He told Mrs. Stein that he thought it strange that Don De Vargas his brother and the Judge had dinner and then went into Don's private office for many hours. So, Mrs. Stein told Jerry that there was rumor among the Stein's friends that the Judge might be partial to men and women. So, the flood gate opened and Jerry said that was his thinking but he didn't know how she would take it so he didn't exactly bring it into the open.

Mrs. Stein tried all her tricks to get Jerry to be more specific but Jerry said that he never saw a compromising act like kissing or hugging, but they were very close maybe they both were good at discretion. So that being said, we may be able to use Don De Vargas as the other one causing one to divorce. The two lawyers agreed that it was extremely plausible that something was going on and asked Mrs. Stein if she wanted her investigators to try to exploit it. They could use long range telescopic cameras and other high-tech tricks as they had no way into the property. It was a long shot but it might work. They agreed to meet again in two weeks unless something broke and broke it did. The head attorney called Mrs. Stein and said that Don De Vargas and the Judge were seen and photographed putting luggage in Don De Vargas's Lincoln continental and driving away together. The investigators were trailing were this go we will have to see. The trail was to begin in one week. Mrs. Stein did not have any real concrete pieces of evidence it was mostly assumable as possible. Mrs. Stein's lawyers filed an affidavit proclaiming that Judge Stein had a significant other and it was a male a Mr. Don De Vargas. The press went wild and it was headlines in all the major newspapers and magazines. It was a very traumatic experience for Don De Vargas and Judge Stein. Now Don De Vargas was in the picture. Judge Stein's lawyers filed for a change of dates for the trial to begin as they needed time to explore this new accusation. The presiding Judge gave them five more days and that was quite a shock. The Democratic Party was hurt beyond question.

Their front runner for Governor of Wyoming, Judge Stein was just blown out of the water. Judge Stein was also the Democratic front runner for next presidential election. So, if Judge Stein won the governor's race, he was s shoe in for the presidential race. One thing led to another. Should De Vargas and Judge Stein agree to a settlement out of court? Judge Stein and his father were both exceptional attorneys so they knew the game. Throw out your fishing line and see if you catch something. They also knew that that if they settled out of court that there would be many, many people that would regard that as an act of guilt. So, the decision was to fight on. The bombshell that Mrs. Stein set off was hurting Isaac Stein not only because of the Judges reputation but because of business commitments and relationships. So, the bizarre happenings were so to speak killing two birds with one stone. Carl said to Donald, let me explain.

Mr. Isaac Stein was presently in the process of expanding into Nevada County. The plan was on the drawing board for some time, but Mr. Stein did not seem to think that it needed to go all out but to gradually develop the new plan. But things change. The trial would hold up Isaac Stein's plans even if he had a mind to accelerate his plan, but again things changed for Mr. Stein. He had received a call from his land broker and the broker came upon some land that was too good to pass up. There was a total of two hundred thousand acres mostly flat and ideal for sheep or cattle. The land was being probated so it would be a while before it came up for bid. Much of Nevada at that time was undeveloped and desert land so the prospects of a land rush were out and the exorbitant cost of developing, sewage and water. It would require deep pockets but the ultimate reward would be monstrous. The land also had some natural perks such as the mountains provided a good quantity of water.

As much of Nevada was desert that was a big plus. Another favorable asset the land offered was that with the huge amount of acreage, other enterprises saw large gains if they worked with the hug gains if they worked with Mr. Stein, one such corporation was the railroad system. The rails provided ranches cheap reliable transportation for the product, so that was huge. Mr. Stein liked what he heard and wished that it would have come into the open six months ago. In business one day sometimes can make or break your most fantastic plans. Although there were many obstacles, Mr. Stein agreed to tie up the property and wait for his opportunities. The trail itself had not started as each party wanted more time. Each camp was trying its darndest to find something, anything. Judge Stein was a more stand up man so Mrs. Stein's lawyers could not reasonably find much to work with. On the other hand, Don De Vargas was a people person and a party man as such was much more the prime target. Don DeVargas was also an astute business man and was always on the job. So, after weeks of frustration and not hitting a home run. Mrs. Stein and her attorneys could not connect the dots. Furthermore, if she did not win this case Don De Vargas's lawyers said they would counter with a one-million-dollar suit against Mrs. Stein. Judge Stein's lawyers made the same vow. Judge Stein lawyers sensed that they had Mrs. Stein and her lawyers on the run so they told the presiding Judge that they were ready to proceed with the trial. The case came to an abrupt halt.

When Mrs. Stein's lawyers told the opposing lawyers that they were willing to drop all charges and to assume all court and lawyer costs, the opposing lawyers were not going to let them off the hook so easily because a lot of damage was done. They demanded a public apology on national television and her wish to be divorced would not be a contested with these provisions. She would have two months to vacate Mr. Isaac Stein's property. No compensation was to be made to Mrs. Stein. All parties agreed, papers were signed and the trail was over before it began. But as we shall see what's over is not necessarily over. Yes, the Judge and Don De Vargas won but sometimes winning is losing as in the case of Judge Stein. The trial was so emotionally draining that the Judge being so devastated that he proclaimed to his superiors that he would not seek to campaign for Judgeship and that he would not be a candidate for president where that was due. Judge Stein had six or months to fulfill his Judgeship and he let the powers know that he intended to fill out his commitment. So, Judge Stein's life would be changed forever.

The plan was for Judge Stein to wind down slowly and restart his engine so to speak. He would than devote himself to politicking charity work or whatever came to mind. On the other hand, Mr. Isaac Stein had his work cut out for him. Isaac decided to go gung-ho on his new venture. Number one priority was to live on the new property no more commuting back and forth. So being that the property was undeveloped and he needed a place to live. He bought an elaborate motorhome that was self-contained with bedrooms, bathrooms, kitchen and living space neatly arranged so it was comfortable. He rented a portable office that adjourned his motor home. That being done he set down in earnest and planned his scheme what was to be done first and what could wait.

His first thought was to hire some carpenters and build a large structure for mechanical apparatuses such as jeeps, trailers and heavy-duty trucks so that he had transportation. Mr. Stein had his new Cadillac but it was not conducive to training the property. Next he hired a helicopter as to fly him over the whole of his land so he could see firsthand what could be here and what could be there. Donald was getting a bit edgy so he asked Carl what all his had to do with the politics of electing a president. Carl assured Donald it was all a preview of what was to come. Mr. Bizzar was not done with the Stein's he was never done as we shall see. So, Carl continued. Mr. Bizzar entered this arena with nostrils bellowing smoke and flame.

He was a giant player, he never played favorited everyone and everything was his playground. On one of his aerial trips they saw a sort of tent city. This was a shock and worth investigating. Mr. Stein's preliminary notices did not disclose this fact. So, Mr. Stein had his pilot land the helicopter so they could clear some of the fog. What was discovered was a small village of American Indians. These people lived here for many decades. The tribe was a peaceful family-oriented tribe. Mr. Stein talked to the chief. The chief said that the ongoing president set a precedent that deeded fifty acres to the tribe. It was all legally done and the chief showed Mr. Stein copies of the title.

Mr. Stein had no objections in fact he was pleased that this happened, but he was disappointed that the fact was not presented to him but it had to bite him. Mr. Stein was oriented as a lawyer to try to always have the facts before him so that there were no surprises. Suffice to say that the chief was offering Mr. Stein a very valuable asset. Members of his tribe, traveled and recorded much useful information regarding Mr. Stein's property. This first-hand information would have taken Mr. Stein and his team of workers many hours or days of relentless work to ascertain where there might be water where the best prospects to build certain amenities such as a small dam so that they would have proper water systems. The Indians knew land like none else because they lived by land from their beginning. Mr. Stein and the chief agreed to work together, which they did, to develop the property into a profitable entity. This took about one year of hard work and many millions of dollars but the end result was terrifying mind boggling what was achieved. Mr. Stein's dream was coming true. Not only was this the biggest most modern ranch in Nevada, but the prosperity and employment for the area was unbelievable. The ranch and its pledge to the community took Nevada from a desolate state to prosperity. Nevada would never again be where you went to divorce never again be just a glitz and gambling state. It was a state to be reckoned with. Mr. Stein's personal reward was the pleasure of committing a small portion of his acreage to cattle but only on a hobby basis. His first love was sheep as he studied sheep and was successful in raising sheep, but he loved the idea of some prize head of cattle to try and cultivate a herd of specialty animals. She bought some Belgian cattle and like his sheep the hobby was taking hold of him and soon he had a formidable herd of cattle.

Everything he touched seemed to be exploding with success but his Nevada ranch was a sheep ranch and not a cattle and sheep ranch. He was forced once again to come up with some answers. It came about in Arizona. Mr. Black and his wife ran and owned a small specialty ranch for breeding different species of cattle. Mr. Stein and Mr. Black became friends when Mr. Black sold Mr. Stein his first heads of Belgian cattle. So, Mr. Stein called his friend. Mrs. Black received the call and she was very happy to hear from Mr. Stein. Mrs. Black had to tell Mr. Stein that her husband had passed away and she was left with the ranch and its many heads of cattle.

Mrs. Black was not a rancher but the wife of a rancher. The small ranch would be neglected very soon as she had no intention of continuing on with that business. She asked Mr. Stein if he knew of someone that would purchase the ranch. Mr. Stein said that he would drive down to see her and talk to her about buying it. Mrs. Black was very grateful and hung up. Mr. Stein drove to the ranch the following day. Mr. Stein was familiar with the ranch as he had several occasions to meet with Mr. Black. Mrs. Black invited Mr.

Stein to dinner and during dinner they discussed the problems surrounding Mrs. Black. Mr. Stein said he would buy the ranch but he wanted to see what was left of the inventory. Mrs. Black was selling off the cattle a bit at a time.

Mr. Stein said he made reservations at a nearby hotel and he would see her tomorrow at about ten a.m. and he left. The following day he talked to some realtor's that specialized in sales of ranches. He wanted to get a ball park figure in his mind as to what a rundown ranch would be worth. He got some answers, some absurd ad some practical so he had to read between the lines and draw a conclusion. If a realtor was oblivious as to the condition of the ranch home or the barns and property in general all he could tell Mr. Stein that assuming the house, assuming the barns and the shape of the remaining cattle he would say it was worth so and so if he assumed everything was respectfully maintained or if he assumed it was totally neglected than that presented a different light on the price. Mr. Stein by nature of his experience was probably much more knowledgeable about land and business that the people he was trying to get to advise him. So actually, it was an act of futility to even consider that it made sense to contact these people. So, he arrived at Mrs. Black's home and they sat down to coffee and Danish and visited for a while.

Finally, Mr. Stein told Mrs. Black of his conversations with the reality firms. He sincerely wanted to be fair about what to offer Mrs. Black. Money was no object, but you had to live with your actions. Mrs. Black was fairly naïve about the ranch business. She was utterly beyond her scope of reality at this moment in her life in other words she was very vulnerable. Whatever sounded right to her at this moment in time was acceptable just so she could get out of the mess with dignity. Mr. Stein was her best option. Her former husband said he was by far the fairest man he ever dealt with. So, with that in mind she accepted Mr. Stein's offer with no haggling and no down the middle just as it was. To be fair, Mr. Stein gave her much more than the property was worth, but he had no regrets. So, he gave Mrs. Black a check and said he would pick her up tomorrow at ten a.m. and they would go to the bank and finalize the deal so that he would get a clear title and legal recording. He told Mrs. Black that she could take her time moving out but would it be all right for him to send two or three men over to start caring for the animals. Mrs. Black said for him to assume she wasn't there and to bring his men to do their job. When Mrs. Black and Mr. Stein first began doing business, Mr. Stein asked Mr. Black for a person that he might suggest to one to Nevada and help him get started with the cattle. Mr. Black said he had a young man that would suit him fine and his name was Brad Worth. Brad Worth was a graduate of a respectable college in California and he was a registered veterinarian. Brad did not like to be holed up in some office tending to animals. He wanted to work on a ranch. Brad came to work for Mr. Stein. They both respected what they had so when there is unity life in general is so much easier. So, Mr. Stein played out his hobby and Brad made his hobby and Brad made his hobby profitable. So, Mr. Stein called the ranch in Nevada and spoke with Brad and told him to pick two or three men and with a couple of trucks to come to the Black ranch.

Brad knew of the ranch as he worked for Mr. Black. Brad arrived with three more men and Mr. Stein told Brad that he was to be the big honcho. He wanted the place to shine bright. You will have a blank check to do this right. Mr. Stein had some business to attend to and if anything, big comes along to contact him. Mr. Stein said I'll try and be back here in about two weeks. In the meantime, Mrs. Black moved into town and shortly she bought a small cottage and was very content. There were two underdeveloped properties of one hundred acres each bordered the Black ranch and he made offers for both of them, but he did not hear from the realtor so he told Brad to call him if something transpired.

Carl feeling guilty told Donald that Arizona had no relationship to our discussion but got carried away and threw it in there for whatever it was worth. So, Mrs. Stein drove back to the ranch in Nevada. You will see Donald how Bizzar moves from one thing to without missing a beat. Mr. Stein liked to drive big cars like Cadillac's or Lincoln Continental's and he owned both. He felt secure when he leisurely drove from one ranch to the other. Nowadays executives deemed that mode of transportation was obsolete. But Mr. Stein was old school and he liked to drive while driving he would relax and analyze and ponder the question of life. Life in general has been good to him and his family so he took pleasure in slowing down and sort of reminiscing while he was driving.

This one particular trip took him to Reno, Nevada where there he met with his sheep buyers and transacted whatever business on hand. He was very pleased with the results of this latest transaction but now he was again faced with the problem of time. He was always thinking and moving so after a big deal he usually had to push himself to slow down. He had a good meal, played some games and found out that nothing was working as far as slowing down was concerned. He couldn't sleep so he decided to move along, so he and his Cadillac were reunited. Sometimes he like to drive relatively obscure roads so that he could drive the way some drivers pushed you to drive at their speed. So, he was on this more or less secluded road. The only other vehicle that he noticed was a black pickup about a mile behind him. It was keeping pace with his speed. So, Mr. Stein slowed down figuring the pickup would pass him, but no, the pickup also slowed down. So, the two played the game of fast and slow but always with the pickup in back of him.

By now, Mr. Stein was getting very apprehensive. He was driving an obscure road and it was two a.m. His phone was not picking up any signals so it was dead. He also had about fifty thousand dollars in cash in the satchel on the floorboard of the car. He now was convinced that the black pickup was trailing him to probably find the right moment to make his move and rob him. He was no convinced that the driver of the pickup was there by design not by coincidence. His son, Judge Stein often berated his father for always having a lot of cash on hand, but Mr. Stein was old school and he told his son that cash was king. Hysteria started to set in, Mr. Stein was elderly and hypertension was causing him some discomfort. Mr. Stein had driven this route a few times so he knew the road to some degree. His mind was trying to tell him where the driver of the pickup would make his move. Up ahead was a series of curves that would slow him down. That surely would be a good spot to force him off the road. Just around the first bend he blacked out. At that moment the driver of the pickup could not see the Cadillac as it was already in the cure of this slightly hilly stretch of road. The driver of the pickup occasionally came to Reno and had used this same road and he liked the slower pace as did Mr. Stein. Suddenly he noticed a big fireball of light just beyond the curve of the hill. He accelerated his truck when he also saw smoke. He guessed it was an accident and he was right. The Cadillac was flipped on its side and grass fires were around the car, probably from gas spewing out of the motor. The Cadillac must have flipped four or five times as it was quite a way removed from the road.

He parked his pickup, but made sure it was far enough away so that it would not be in anger in case the car exploded. He dashed down to the overturned car, the car itself was not on fire, but the small grass fires would get worse so he had very little time. The car laid on the driver's side. He tried to open the doors, but they were either locked or jammed by the flipping. He was an avid camper so he had a box full of tools useful for camping such as pliers, a hatchet, and a hammer. So, he went back to his pickup and got a hatchet and a bedroll and a few blankets also a small fire extinguisher. He ran back to the care and used the fire extinguisher to put out the flames near the car. Then he used the hatchet to break out the windshield. He carefully placed a blanket over the frame of the opening. He climbed into the car and there was an elderly man covered in blood.

The man was unconscious but he was breathing quite normally. He was alive. He was still in his seat belt that had jammed as he could not release it. He being a camper always had with him a sturdy knife that he used to cut the seatbelt strap. The car was getting very hot and he figured he did not have much time before the fire would ignite the gas tank the dilemma was that the man was unconscious and the only way out was through the windshield opening all the doors were jammed. Fortunately, the old man was not overly large so maybe he could leverage him out of the car through the windshield opening, but he was in fairly good shape so that he might be able to wrestle him out of the car. He did not have much time as the flames were getting hotter and hotter.

He was not strong enough to pull the man from behind the steering wheel and the only way was to get under him and slid him out. That worked, he got him out through the window but when he pushed the old man so he could get out the old man rolled off the hood onto the ground. Luckily there was no grass burning there. He crawled out and dragged the old man a considerable distance from the grass fire and covered the man with a blanket. He ran back to the car as when he was wrestling and trying to get the old man out, he saw the satchel and he thought it might have been papers identifying who he was. So, he retrieved the satchel and put it out of harm's way.

He thought it might be prudent to pull the man further from the accident which he did. He figured that the flames would attract a passing plane or some cars on some other road. It was very dark so the fire stood out significantly. Sure, enough it wasn't long before some forest rangers came driving a four-wheel jeep. When they came upon the scene, they radioed the police and ambulance. They then proceeded to put out the flames as they have some very large fire extinguishers strapped to the jeep. A helicopter from Reno arrived and he had two medics that quickly checked out Mr. Stein and they put him some oxygen and other life saving devices. The medics assured everyone that Mr. Stein was going to live but he had several broken ribs, nose and other bruises.

They searched for identification but could not find any. The pickup driver remembered the satchel and he brought it to the helicopter crew. The police finally arrived as the helicopter was leaving. The officer obtained a brief rundown about the events. The truck driver identified himself as Chad Beeham and that he was an attorney from Cheyenne, Wyoming and that he was in Reno for a couple of days. He told the officer about the accident and how he rescued Mr. Stein. He also took pictures of the scene for the police to examine. When the helicopter landed at the hospital, Mr. Stein was examined and hospitalized for further examination. The satchel was given to a nurse to accompany Mr. Stein as yet no one knew the contents of fifty thousand dollars was being juggled around. The police came to the hospital to try to get some identification of the man. The nurse gave the officer the satchel which they opened and nearly fell over as it was full of money. In a pocket of the satchel they found a wallet that had Mr. Stein's identification card. Holy smokes, the driver's license identified him as Isaac Stein. Everyone in Wyoming and Nevada knew or heard of him. Within a matter of minutes after the press was notified, Chad Beeham became one of the most famous persons in Reno. Television stations, radio and all news stations were gathering information to get his story out. The stories erupted into "Lawyer saves Mr. Isaac Stein" and a full page of events was to follow. Others said "Lawyer saves Nevada and Wyoming's Sheep industry story after story went on. Carl told Donald that he had his father were rushed to the Reno hospital. They interviewed Chad and wanted to get firsthand the complete run down of what had happened.

The hero, Chad Beeham was twenty-seven years old. He was a practicing attorney out of Cheyenne, Wyoming. He had his own practice as he did not want to be an attorney for some big cochleate. When he graduated from law school, he got his license to practice law in the state of Wyoming. He loved sports and played some football and participated is some track and field, but he was never a star or of the caliber to pursue the sports in college or professionally. He called himself inadequate. He was only about five six or five seven in height and about one hundred and fifty-four pounds soaking wet. His father was an artist and he worked at a large department store in Cheyenne. He was in the advertisement department of the paper.

His father loved motorcycles and he loved to consume alcohol and the two did not mix to well together. His motorcycle of choice was an old Indian cycle. One evening after consuming too much liquor, he lost control of his motorcycle and hit a series of thirty-gallon garbage cans. The police arrived and he was arrested for driving under the influence. He went to court and was given thirty days in jail because he was also driving on a suspended license. That suspension was also due to a DUI. The department store that Chad's father worked for immediately terminated his employment. He served his sentence and when he got out of jail, he asked his employer if he could be reinstated. He was a very skilled artist so they let him return to work with certain conditions kind of a probation, you do it again and your history. The insurance on the motorcycle was intact so the Indian was repaired.

Chad's father had no driver's license so he gave the Indian to his son, Chad. On pleasant day, Chad drove his father work and picked him up. Other days, Chad's father used public transportation. Chad was an avid camper and he would tie his sleeping bag on his Indian and off he would go. On one such trip he recalls he got into an accident with his motorcycle. The motorcycle hit a slick spot in the road and he flew off. Luckily, he was heavily padded with his father's black leather jacket. He also had on his helmet. When he was thrown, he landed in such a way as to break his ankle. The x-rays showed the break was more severe than a first prognosis. The doctors had to do surgery and place stainless steel pins in his ale. The doctor said that he would walk with a slight limp but that he would eventually walk. While he was recuperating in the hospital, the fourteen-year-old Chad got some more bad news.

His father committed suicide by hanging himself in their garage. Life was a bear for him at age fourteen he had no parents and in he was in the hospital. He was released from the hospital. Chad was not a quitter and he would bounce back but there were momentous times for him. Luckily, he found a job as a carpenter, but he had to work full-tie now which meant that he had to leave school. In order for Chad to get his high school diploma, he was forced to attend night school. Long, long hours ensued. The small house that his father inherited was deeded to Chad. It was little more than a shack but it was in a fairly nice neighborhood and the lot was worth ore that the house. The roof had a leak and there was dry rot and the house needed painting inside and out but it was paid for and he had a roof over his head. Working as a carpenter led him to acquire the necessary skills to repair the house, money permitting. He put on a new shingle roof. He finished his night school and got his high school diploma but it was winter and carpentry was not in as big a demand so Chad was working about twenty hours a week. He finally got a break as the high school principal ha a brother that was a lawyer. Chad was offered a part time job for three days a week to be as assistant to the lawyer. Chad was now eighteen years old. The lawyer was very impressed with Chad's work ethics and hat prompted the lawyer to ask Chad if he had any desire to attend college to become an attorney. Chad of course said yes but he did not have the funds at this time to do this. The lawyer said that he would obtain a loan for him and that he would sign the note. Chad agreed to the note and now he was off to college to become a lawyer. Chad worked in the evenings and weekends for his lawyer friend.

Sometimes he filled in for his former contractor boss. It was tough indeed but Chad managed to persevere. He kept his head above water, but just barely and he also knew that there would be light at the end of the tunnel. He finally finished college and got his lawyers certificate. He passed his bar examination and just like that he was a lawyer. Chad was used to adversity so he would continue along that path. He decided that he would work for himself knowing that again he would be struggling. Chad had a sign made that simply said Carl Beeham, Attorney. He used one of his bedrooms for his office and he was in business with no clients. Chad was proud of what he had accomplished.

His first case finally came his way. It was from his former contractor boss. It so happened that one of his carpenters cut off two of his fingers and his ex-boss let his workman's compensation insurance lapse so he was being sued by the injured worker. Chad managed to settle the case for his former boss, but it wasn't cheap, the settlement at least let his ex-boss keep his contractor's license and stay in business. Chad's first case was a draw but things were looking up. Chad did not make much money but he was happy that he could help out his ex-boss.

Chad's second and third cases were easier and he was drawing up living trusts also for some families. Some of these cases were straight forward legality and did not require any court appearances, it was all job experience with little or no pay. He was busy and generally pleased with himself. Chad finally came to a position that he could afford to treat himself. He just concluded a good case so goodbye Cheyenne and put out a notice that he was going fishing and to contact his answering service and he would be back in three days. He was enjoying himself camping, fishing and just literally laying back, but after three days he got antsy and he wanted to get back to work.

So, he packed up his sleeping bad and cooking utensils, strapped them to the Indian and he was soon on the road heading home. Time has a way of passing by and he was now twenty-seven-years-old. Chad's life took on a feeling of boredom or standing still, soldiers called it marching in place. One case was good, when another was ho hum. Chad was systematically building a good solid base. He never got a homerun case that could set him up a bit so head to plug along each day. To tell the truth, that's the way he wanted his business to be. Otherwise he would not be able to go out and camp and do the things he loved. He knew he could work fifty to sixty hours a week and bring in a lot more money. One day his neighbor lady came and she brought him a piece of chocolate cake and a sandwich. She was an elderly woman of German dissent. She was born in America and went to school in the America but her accent was such as it was barely distinguishable. When Chad's mother and father were alive, they often traded off doing dinners together. Her name was Gretchen and she was married to a Latin man that was stout. His trade was auto mechanics and he was by far the best. His name was Enrico and he worked for the largest auto agency in Cheyenne, but his true love was cooking his Mexican food. He cooked tacos, enchiladas, tamales there were always superbly done. Enrico would have had little trouble changing occupations but he also loved automobiles. Greyhen's house was always filed with goodies, which his house had none. Enrico was a superb cook but Gretchen's specialty was sauerbraten.

When it came time for Chad's father and mother to treat them always went out as Chad's mother was not a very good cook and Chad's father could not eve boil water. They always went to a little Chinese place that was hole in the wall but they know how to cook. Many specialties included Pot Sticker's, Mongolian Beef, Chow Mein all the dishes were truly delicious. One day Gretchen came to his office to ask if dog could sit for their gold cocker spaniel as she was leaving for Wisconsin to care for her ailing sister. Well Chad had never had a dog but he figures that he could learn to do the job. Gretchen figured to be one for at least a week. Chad loved dog sitting and he vowed to get a dog when Gretchen returned. Chad would take the spaniel for a walk each evening and that is how he met Madeline an as it happened, she was to become his wife.

On his evening walks, the cocker spaniel would take the lead and he would follow. The dog knew if she directed Chad, she could lead him to Tarantino's market where all the tantalizing smells were coming from. Tarantino's market was one of three buildings in the small strip mall owned by Giuseppe and his wife. The market was the largest building and then there was a Chinese laundry, dry cleaner and next to that was a pharmacy that had a little soda fountain and it was the local hangout for the high school kids. The high school was only about two blocks away. So, if the cocker spaniel turned left, we just walked as there were no strip malls or stores strictly a residential area.

At the end of that street was a gorgeous two-story Victorian home owned or formerly owned by Mrs. & Mrs. Eric Sorenson or Doctor Sorenson. Husband and wife were both physicians and they were now retired and about eight years old. When they passed away the Victorian was put up for bid and Madeline's mother bought the home. Madeline's family was from Rhode Island and Madeline's mother opened a high-end boutique. Madeline worked for her mother. There was another younger sister and she was a gifted artist. The younger sister was known as a professional student as she was always attending art schools.

Madeline's mother was diagnosed as having lung cancer and her physician suggested that she move to a warmer state so she sold the boutique and moved to Arizona. They lived in Arizona for about one year but Madeline's mother did not like it in Arizona so they moved to Cheyenne, Wyoming and eventually bought the Victorian. The home was to be remodeled and made into a unique upscale boutique, but shortly after that Madeline's mother passed away, so Madeline was heir to the extensive remodeling and the great task of procuring whatever was need for the boutique. When the cocker spaniel and I got to the Victorian, there was a crew of painters inside. The place was lit up like a Christmas tree so I was totally amazed as this was the first time that I witnessed so much light and goings on at the Victorian. The hustle and bustle were such that I was unaware of other going on. Madeline got out of her car. I did not know her then and she looked at me and said "Curiosity killed the cat" she looked at him and giggled in amusement that she had startled him. When I came to my senses, I turned towards her and said "you're beautiful". Then there was another bell like giggle and she apologized for frightening me. They both stared at each other like a couple of kids, grownup kids so that was when and how Chad met Madeline.

    Chad would love that dog forever for turning the right way and introducing the two of them to a lifetime of love and reverence for each other. Chad introduced himself and Madeline did the same. Chad was in love and he talked about nothing. It finally came out that he was dog sitting the neighbor's dog. Madeline loved animals so she sat on the cold sidewalk and petted and talked dog talk to the cocker spaniel. She asked the spaniel what her name was to this day Chad had no idea of how Madeline knew his name was Senior Cocker. Did the dog blurt it out or did he? Somethings are left to be forgotten. Madeline again giggled and Chad knew somehow, he would hear that bell like giggle for the rest of his life. Madeline stood up and told Chad that Senior cocker was the most beautiful dog she had ever had the pleasure of meeting. She asked if she could take the leash and walk Senior Cocker while she and Chad could talk. Chad told Madeline that he was an attorney and lived about a block down this same street.

    His practice was in a part of the home and he resided in the other. Madeline told Chad about her mother's chic boutique and the sad affair of her mother passing away. Madeline's step father was a vice president of an upscale woman's shoe company and he was going to stock her boutique with the shows and she would have an exclusive line of woman shoes? If all went well her step father said that she could be the West Coast distributor. Madeline's sister's name was Alice and she was an artist. Alice inherited the same as did Madeline but she was not interested in the boutique so she was a silent partner. Madeline told Chad about how they ended up in Cheyenne, Wyoming. Alice loved to attend art class and one of the girls she met was from Cheyenne. During a summer break one of the girls said she was going home to Cheyenne. She lived with her mother. Her parents were divorced. Usually when she had summer break she would live and visit with her father. She asked Alice if she would like to come and visit at her father's ranch for a couple of weeks.

Her father's ranch was a medium size ranch that boarded and trained horses for shows. They also breeded horses for riding shows and racing horses. She was quite successful. Alice's friend knew that Alice had an older sister and Madeline was invited to stay one week-end. She liked Cheyenne very much and convinced her ailing mother to move to Cheyenne from Arizona. So, Cheyenne it was. They rented at first and found a nice cottage near the Victorian and that was home.

The Victorian boutique was to be named "Madeline's Boutique" and so here I am. Madeline asked Chad if he was a notary and the answer was no, but his part time bookkeeper was a notary and coincidently would be in the office tomorrow which was Monday. Her name was Memphis Navarro and she worked from nine to twelve for Chad. Madeline told Chad that she would be at his office on Monday at 10:00 a.m. Without further ado Chad and Madeline left each other.

Chad physically left but his mind was reeling. He did not know how to handle the feelings he was experiencing. He hoped Madeline was feeling the same. Madeline and Chad both had very restless experiences that evening but they both survived. At ten a.m. Madeline was at Chad's office. Chad introduced Madeline to Memphis and left the two to do their private business, and he to do his thing. Madeline was surprised when she Memphis because she had envisioned a young voluptuous pretty girl, maybe about twenty-five years old. Instead Memphis was an older lady probably about sixty years old. She was an American Indian with long silver hair, a cooper complexion. She had a slight hooked nose that enhanced her look all in all she was rather pretty. When the shock was over for Madeline, the two set about doing their business. After their business was done, Memphis asked Madeline if they could have lunch together in the near future. They both agreed that Thursday coming would fit both their schedules. The two exchanged phone numbers and said that they would talk further. Madeline paid her bill and left the office. Chad called her and asked if was available for lunch. Madeline had to decline as she said it was a very hectic day. Of course, Chad was devastated, but it was short lived as Madeline called him later and apologized for being so blunt. She was having a showing of dresses and apparel and there were five difference sales representatives all trying to get Madeline's business. It was so daunting. The representatives all knew about Madeline's mother's success with her boutique back east and they envisioned the same at Madeline's Boutique in Cheyenne. If there was going to be success, they all wanted to be a part of it. Madeline than sent Chad to the moon, she asked if they could have dinner tomorrow evening. They agreed to have Italian as Madeline and her mother both enjoyed a certain Italian restaurant that had excellent food. They agreed that seven p.m. would be fine and Chad would pick her up at her home. Tan reality set in. The reality was transportation. He had an Indian motorcycle plus a heap of a pick-up truck not a carriage with six horses. Lady luck was with him.

Gretchen his neighbor had a new Buick plus her deceased husband's new black pickup and she asked Chad if he would mind starting the vehicles up so as the batteries would not go dead. She gave Chad the keys and said for him to use the vehicles if needed, problem solved. Whew! When they arrived at the restaurant they were seated in a private booth and menus were presented. The Italian menus could have been in Greek or Chinese as far as Chad was concerned. He had to bluff his way out and he asked Madeline to order so she said she wanted Calamari Fritti with Risotto and spinach. Chad took the easy way out. He proclaimed her would have the same as her. The meal was excellent and the conversation stimulating as they were both trying to get to know more about each other.

Chad realized that life, real life was passing him by, and if it were not for Madeline he would be working until ten p.m. And probably had sandwiches of sorts and the next day, resume the same old same old. Chad did not know woman, but he knew that Madeline was two years younger than he and her sister Alice was four years younger that she was. Could he keep this woman as his own? Chad was by no means illiterate to life, but was more devoted to a life of work, work for what? Chad did not cherish money or want anything in a grand way. He just wanted to be the best attorney he could e and let every other thing be there and not be these. Chad told Madeline about his mother and father. He could not remember his mother to well as he was quite young. His mother died of natural causes that were never really discussed with Chad.

His father was an artist that could not get a grip on life without his wife. He subsequently committed suicide. In his wallet he had a short note from his father. He handed it to Madeline to read. It read, "My son had, excused me for leaving you like this, but life without your mother is unbearable". Love you always, Dad. Madeline told Chad her real father was killed in a skiing accident when he collided with a tree during a blinding snow storm. Her mother had a successful boutique back east. She was diagnosed with lung cancer and subsequently dies just recently.

To break the atmosphere, Madeline told Chad that she liked Memphis, Chad's booker very much and that they were to have lunch together tomorrow. Chad told Madeline that Memphis was a math prodigy and a professional chess master. She participated all over the world competing with the giants of the world of chess. It all ended abruptly when she started drinking and losing matches that under normal circumstances she would have easily won. So, she became an accountant and was content to have a lesser life but a meaningful life. So again, Madeline had to change the subject so she remarked about liking his new Buick and that her father was partial to Buicks. Chad than had to tell Madeline the circumstances that evolved into his having the Buick tonight.

The evening was slipping by and the waiter excused himself and said that they were ready to close the restaurant for the day and he presented Chad with the bill which he paid and then they left. All in all, it was a perfect evening. He had drove Madeline home and there was a light kiss and hug and a general reluctnesss to have the energy and that was three years ago. Since then, Chad's lawyer business became very fruitful and successfully in fact if it kept going at this pace Chad would be forced to either hire another attorney to take part of the load off and he would have to slow down.

Madeline's boutique was equally successful and it was the I place for many people that were regarded as affluent. Madeline had a very businesslike approach to make the boutique unique to a very assorted segment in Cheyenne. Madeline held showings that the various dress manufacturer liked to think we're going to be the rage this year. She had little lunches for a variety of society. All in all, the boutique was a big success. Chad still liked to go fishing and camping and he and Madeline liked to go to Reno and Las Vegas to simply let everything go for three or four days.

During that span of three years, Alice got married to an art instructor in Paris, France. Since than the couple moved to New York City. They now had a lovely daughter presenting Madeline with her first relative. It seems like change comes and goes forever. Carl was getting tired so he told Donald that he would continue the Chad story tom morrow. There was a lot more to Chad than the first introduction presented. The next day, Carl, Donald, Jeremiah and Martha were having a pleasant breakfast. Carl told Donald that he was completely refreshed and that if Donald liked they could resume were they left off.

Donald knew that Carl would exploit every facet of his and Donald's father's exclusive interview with Chad Chesham. Forget that it might pertain to side stories. Carl knew that every little event had its place in a story and if they were omitted eventually the story changed. Carl learned that very early in his long career as a writer. In the end, Carl's stories always came together were as you might think he was rambling on but not on the subject matter of President of the U.S. Carl and he proceeded to the hospital where Mr. Stein were recuperating. Former Judge Stein was there at his father's bedside. Carl asked the hospitals permission to interview Mr. Stein.

The hospitals general manager new of Carl's and my father's reputation so in general he had no misgivings to agree with Carl's request. He the hospital manager also had is play, in play. Carl would write him and hospital in very good light so the general public and his superiors would be impressed at the hospitality being extended to one of Nevada's favorites. Mr. Stein came out of his accident in very favorable circumstances. He was treated for shock and exposure. He had minor bruises, plus a broken nose also two ribs were broken. X-rays showed no concussions and no further complications so Mr. Stein was extremely lucky the main reason being his age. If Mr. Stein would not have been more or less a health person, he might have succumbed to the severity of the accident itself. Carl and my father let Mr. Stein tell his story. Mr. Stein admits that his thoughts were along the likes of an ambush, robbery and possibly murder, but he was terribly wrong. As the whole world knew. Never before in all his travels was, he ever as conscious of a peril lurking to cause him harm. All he knew was that the shiny black pick-up was always there in his rear-view mirror. So, the natural result was that the hypertension caused him to black out. That's the extent of my knowledge. What Chad told you was beyond me as I was unconscious. So, between Chad's accounting and Mr. Stein, Carl and my father were able to report a Pulitzer story. If the two journalists were not the most liked and sought-after journalist in the world, they sure would be so now.

So, Carl and my father left Mr. Stein and Judge Stein. Judge Stein was not an active participating Judge any longer but he would always be called Judge Stein. Chad and Madeline received a call from the hospital that Mr. Stein and his son would like to see him and offer thanks as this was the first opportunity that presented itself, he was up to his neck in the hands of the doctors until just recently. So, the four set about greeting each other and thanking. Judge Stein held up his arms and said that the Stein Family wanted to present Chad with money. The amount was more than Chad could possibly make as a small attorney. They asked Chad to be one of Mr. Stein's lead attorneys. In other words, they offered Chad the moon. Chad could have asked for anything and it would have been gratefully given to Chad. Chad was overwhelmed, but refused it all. He was not being modest but he had Madeline and for him that was enough. Chad said that any normal person would have done what he did. Chad said maybe thank you was in order but not much more. The police, the medics and the Steins were not as complacent as Chad as they thought that it would not have been an unreasonable premise that someone other than Chad would have taken the satchel full of money and left the scene of the accident. With no regrets. Mr. Stein said that the Judge was going to give Chad and Madeline (Madeline was presented as Chad's fiancé). A "Thank you Chad Party "was soon as Mr. Stein overcame all his injuries. It was quite apparent to Chad and also Madeline that they had a large influx of business and they attributed that to the Stein's popularity. So, the four reminisced about faith and the hands of Mr. Bizzar that under different circumstances it might not have been Chad as the hero or possible the accident night not have happened at all.

Chad had won a very compelling case and what was his policy that when he was so blessed, he ad Madeline would kind of relax and go fishing or camping or both, but this particular time Madeline was up to her neck obligations. She was having a big dress sale and show. The models were already hired and it could not be cancelled. She begged off to Chad and convinced him to do his thing and that she would come to him later. So, everyone knows that did not happen. So, Chad being alone and lonely decided to drive home. The rest is history. So, it was agreed that Chad and Madeline would attend the party that the Steins were setting up. The party came and went and things got back to being reasonably normal. It was now almost a year since the accident. The Steins and Chad and Madeline were very close and whenever it was possible, Chad and Madeline would visit the Stein ranch and just relax and be welcomed. "Okay" Carl said to Donald, "When things go too smoothly, they have to settle back to reality". "Nothing goes straight up or smooth forever". To me this represents the saying calm sea are a prelude to a bad storm and one is coming that I have to tell you about. Your very sight of you says Mr. Bizzar is the prime player but before we get into that we have to consider big payers and what effect they have.

Take for instances Mr. Stein's accident tough it is well in the background these days, because time moves on, but every once in a while, the past seems to pop up whether it's good or bad it's always there. In this case its two pieces of machinery what could two pieces of machinery have to do with the catastrophic accident that ended fairly well indeed. When I talked to Mr. Stein, he brought the subject up and I pondered the facts. Conclusion the presents of these two pieces of machinery were probably the difference between life and death. I am not a very pessimist or optimize individual but sometimes facts present themselves and you have to think, "What if". Okay what if Chad had not been at the scene with his two fire extinguishers, the car rolled multiple times, why did not turn into a fireball? Chad arrived and extinguished enough grass fire near the upturned car so that it did not catch on fire. So that piece of machinery although a common vehicle did not turn into a raging fire or death trap. Mr. Stein also said that the second piece of machinery, in his mind was like big black boggy man ready to gulp him done in one bite. This caused the apparent hypertension that caused Mr. Stein to black out. On the other hand, the black shiny pickup was carrying lifesaving tools that helped or played a big part so the accident was not a fatal one.

Chad always had with him in the pickup the makings for a camping trip at any conceivable time or convenient time. So, he had a hatchet, hammer, knives, blanket at the ready not to say his two fire extinguishers and an overabundance of flares that indecently were seen by passing airplanes that reported the accident. So you have to wonder "What if" Carl said that his career was finished and now he would get on to exploit Mr. Bizzar and the new scenario that was once again going to plague Judge Stein and former Mrs. Stein once again were to be instrumental in showing his hatred for the Steins that would cause the worlds media to proclaim in a few choice words "Judge Stein accused of being a Child Molester" former wife accused Judge Stein of the charge and is suing for twenty-five million dollars. So, the Judge again is in the hot seat. Let's recap a bit. The than Mrs. Stein accused her husband of adultery in her divorce. She ultimately lost the case but was awarded the divorce. So, the former Mrs. Stein was again Miss Sandy Frothing. Sandy inherited a small five-acre estate in Denver Colorado from her parents plus a considerable amount of stock and bonds plus money so she was conceivably one of the most sought of in the society worlds. She was always in the spotlight being the wife of the prominent Judge Stein and the Stein family. At one time, Sandy was a very sought-after model but although she was still a very, very attractive woman that period in her life was passing, but she still kept herself in shape and still attended the society galas that she preferred. Occasionally, Sandy would hold a party or event of her own. At one such party she invited Jerry De Vargas and his brother Don De Vargas. Don De Vargas was the same person she accused of as being the other person her divorce case, which she ultimately lost. Apparently to some people what happened yesterday was old news and soon forgotten.

Sandy was of a type that could hold back her emotions, so that on the outside she appeared to take things in stride, but in reality, they were like a festering sore that never healed. Such was the case of the Stein's, she would never let go, she hated the Stein's and someday somehow, she would have her day in the sun concerning the Stein's. Sandy was a very intelligent person and her fertile brain was always, always contriving different scenarios that would conquer the Steins. She needed a path into that particular part of her life that she lost when she lost her divorce case. She could not fight the Steins from afar she had to be in close range so she could gather the gossip or loose talk that might be relevant. Her scheme was developing although she was not in love with Jerry De Vargas she would tap him in her web and marry him.

Being in the De Vargas camp was about to lose as she could be the Steins as both De Vargas and Stein, and they were the two largest sheep ranchers in Wyoming and they were friendly neighbors and always saw to it that each one was invited to the others gatherings and vice a versa. Sandy catered to Jerry and soon he was so smitten that he asked Sandy to be his wife. Big surprise, no big move forward yes. She was now Mrs. Jerry De Vargas. Under different circumstances, the newlyweds would have lived in Denver at the estate Sandy owned, but Jerry worked at the Vargas ranch and so they were forced to rent for the foreseeable future, but Sandys plan was to eventually live in the mansion that Don De Vargas had built. So, she worked on Jerry. Tell Don De Vargas that you need to be closer to the action so that you would be better at your job. Don De

Vargas was a bachelor and a playboy, but his every move was to enhance the De Vargas sheep business, that was his first love.

Jerry was not a sheep rancher, but he was the firm's chief accountant and although Don De Vargas was not too happy with Jerrys work ethics but he was realistic of the fat that the accounting or business end of the sheep ranch was vitally important so he was very glad to have a motivated brother. Sandy with her skillful maneuvering convinced Don De Vargas that all that happened in the previous defunct divorce case came about due to Judge Stein. She had no intentions of hurting Don De Vargas. So, every available day the Jerry and Sandy De Vargas had dinner with Don De Vargas was she on the right track?

Was she thinking right that the De Vargas and Steins would eventually open the door for her? Personally, it was a long shot, but she did not have too many options. Jerry was not privy to his wife's obsessions as he was in love. Jerry was not very ambitious but with Sandy's prompting he began to realize that his two other brothers were the old men De Vargas favorites so Sandy figures even if the play on the Steins didn't work out, she still had a potential winner in Jerry as he was bound to inherit millions. Not bad Sandy keep it up. Jerry had a son that was afflicted with autism. He lived in a separate room from Jerry and his wife.

His son had a live-in nurse that occupied an adjourning room to his young son Jerrod. By Accident, Sandy got her big break and Jerrod and the nurse were almost nonexistent as far as Jerry and Sandy were concerned. Jerry did not hate his son per say, but he figures that he was given the short end of the stick when it was revealed what Jerrod was ailing from. Jerry and Jerrod never were like father and son. His first wife left him when they lived in Australia and kind of dumped Jerrod into his life as Jerrod's only benefactor. Jerry's ego was flattened as he figured that his first wife was a looser and a druggie and she left him "A De Vargas" for another man which to him as inconceivable. He always regarded Jerrod as being sired by someone else as he had very little relationships with his former wife. Not realizing that it only takes once and once it could have been. For the time being he would let things as they were but as in Sandy's case, he also had demons to suppress. When the time came, he would have some DNA tests done. Sandy's big break came accidently as I said before. One day as Jerry and Sandy were having breakfast Jerrod's nurse came to Jerry and asked if she could be with Jerrod for a few hours as she had a doctor's appointment. Jerry said that he would look in on Jerrod while she was gone. So that opened the door for Jerry and Sandy to discuss Jerrod in-depth as before it was just that Jerrod was his son. They talked about Jerrod's infliction and where it would go from here.

Jerry said that when Judge Stein lived in the guest house, he and Jerrod were very close. Each evening after dinner the Judge would read to young Jerrod. Jerrod loved Judge Stein but I often wondered what the Judge's motives were. Why does a viral man like Judge Stein spend his valuable time with a sick boy? Boy did that ever get Sandy's gears meshing. Sandy called her attorney and they laid out a plan. It was simple, convince Jerrod that Judge Stein was not what he seemed to be. Pound that into the boy's head day in and day out Judge Stein is a pervert, a pervert. Sandy hired the best attorney available to exploit her rights. She, Sandy was very displeased with her former attorneys, they should have convinced the Judge and jury that even though they had no real jarring proof, there were enough circumstantial reasons to win the approval of the jury. For instance, why did the Judge and Don De Vargas go into seclusion after each dinner? The two went into a private room for hours each evening. Of course, Sandy's attorneys did not have the convenience of being part of the family or have a so-called ally that could spy upon the two.

They could only make assumptions and naturally the people, the attorneys were trying to convince they also were making their own assumptions. Seeing as the Sandy's attorneys were unable to exploit this rather relevant issue from afar with binoculars and such it ended up to be a mute trifle to the whole case. Since the trial was over it came to light as to the goings on behind closed doors. It was no sinister dime novel; it was a personal encounter between a client and his attorney. The revealed facts were that Don De Vargas allegedly impregnated one of his man girlfriend's. The girl was an upright person and she fit a normal reason to not send Don De Vargas down the drain. All she wanted was money to assist her in having an abortion, plus enough money so she could start rebuilding her life. Don De Vargas and the Judge were trying to convenience a plan that would not result in a public embarrassment for Don De Vargas, or the girl. The girl was of good family and she was of legal age being twenty years old, so it was a matter of conscious rather than something more sinister. The Judge, Don De Vargas, and the girl were trying to come up with the best solution in a complication dilemma for both Don De Vargas and the girl. Time was of the essence as each day the baby grew and eventually the abortion would be impractical. The outcome was that Don De Vargas gave the girl fifty thousand dollars and set her up in a foreign country to do the abortion, probably Australia where Don De Vargas had connections. So, it was a hush hush meeting each evening to come up with an answer.

Sandy's new attorney was Mr. Fong and he was a no-nonsense attorney that only worked big corporate cases. He seldom was involved in personal cases, unless the dollars made sense. Sandy was sure she would win this time so she offered Mr. Fong exactly what was due him and they signed a contract to that effect. Mr. Fong had a really good team of investigators and Sandy was now in the inner circle of the Don De Vargas mansion life. It wasn't at the debacle of the divorce. So, Mr. Fong figured that as a big positive because now Sandy had complete access to Jerrod and she was quite a striking woman that the young autistic boy didn't have a chance. There were many manly adult males that would attest to that fact. So, every evening she would come to Jerrod's room and work her magic. She had time so she did not pursue Jerrod to the maximum, but her plan was to work on Jerrod until he could not eat or think. It was working well because he told his nurse that he really loved Sandy, but the nurse was not impressed of course Jerrod was only eight years old and could even if he could cope with the wiley Sandy. Another possible bad link was the two De Vargas's. Sandy was married to Jerry De Vargas, Jerrod's father apparently but he had very little backbone in Sandy's estimation so something had to be done with that problem as he might nix the whole plan by not cooperating. Sandy figured she could handle Jerry but Mr. Fong was not so sure. He wanted Jerry out of the picture, the sooner the better. If Jerry said one single complimentary word to Jerrod that the Judge was a good Judge or whatever it might set Sandy's good work back instead of forward. So, Mr. Fong instructed Sandy to play her charms on Don De Vargas as he was always on the hunt and a few choice endearments from Sandy would probably set his ego aloft and his mind was such as to say I want her, I can have her. So, Mr. Fong and Sandy's plan were to convince Don De Vargas to come up with a plan of his own, which would send his brother Jerry home to Australia and butter up the old man De Vargas.

The play unknowing to Jerry was to get in the good graces of the elder De Vargas. In the past, Jerry was not the favorite son he was beset with so many problems that he had a nervous breakdown, the medication and excessive drinking were not helping either. Now Jerry was more or less stable so he would tell his father that his love interest was the family business and he wanted to do all in his power to make amends and work diligently towards that end. The father would be smitten as he always thought Jerry with his compelling knowledge of finances was a plus to his two younger brothers who were excellent ranchers and knew the sheep business but lacked the fine line of finances. Today the elder De Vargas's money was enough so that the two brothers could cope with almost any contingence, but if a major expansion was in order they might possibly be out of their element. That's were Jerry could excel. So, Jerry was sent back home. Sandy now had an open field. Jerrod's nurse was an old timer who went from one household to another as her patients changed. Her mantra was to not concern herself with the families per say but concentrate and do the best for her patient. In the De Vargas household there was evil lurking. She did not know enough to put it all together but she did not rest Sandy one little bit. Sandy would tell her that she could leave the boy in her charge as she Sandy would read to him and stay until Jerrod fell asleep. The nurse would put her ears to the wall and listen, all Sandy did was try to convince Jerrod about the evil Judge Stein. Also, after the evening meal, Don De Vargas and Sandy would go to Don De Vargas's room. They probably were not playing checkers.

The nurse was unaware of the pending court case that Sandy and Mr. Fong were concocting, but she figured something was not right.

She was out of her element. Judge Stein had to be warned. She did not trust the phone systems in the large house she worked in so she drove to the shopping mall and called the Judge. The Judge asked her to come to lunch tomorrow and they would talk, Judge Stein and his father both exceptional attorneys listened to the nurse's assumptions and yes, they agreed something was a foot, but what? They told the nurse to be diligent but careful as they also knew Sandy to be very perceptive and possibly be alert to the fat that Mr. Stein and Judge Stein could smell something was brewing. So, the Judge thanked her and she left. Judge Stein and Mr. Stein figured it best to hire attorneys to try to uncover the plot. The Judge and Isaac Stein still felt indebted to Chad Beeham regarding the accident and they both agreed to let Chad be the lead attorney if he wanted to be. So, Chad and the Stein's met mainly to feel Chad out. As of yet there was no actual litigation but Jerrod's nurse was probably right something was going on, and where Sandy and the Judge are concerned it would not be pleasant. Chad told the Stein's that he would like the opportunity to represent the Stein's and he also told them outright that he was not in the big league with his small practice but he had a lot of confidence in himself that he could step up. He also reminded the Stein's that there were hundreds of attorneys out there that passed the bar, but were not very good. Just because fate brought the Stein's and himself together does not necessarily mean that I am a good attorney. If I happened to be a carpenter because of the accident. It's decent of both of you to try to put me in another bracket and I appreciate it, but also forget loyalty and consider that you have at your fingertips possibly the best attorneys available. Why chance a small one-horse shay above a team of tired and successful attorneys? So, give it plenty of thought. I have no right to think that two of the best attorneys in the land have not already pondered this question. Hopefully there is no case on the horizon and that were being overly sensitive to the fact that a trial is looming. If you will feel better, I will hire some good, reliable investigators to see what they could find out.

Both the Judge and his father agreed so Chad was hired to head off a surprise if it was coming. In the meantime, Sandy was not sitting around and fiddling with her fingers. She was just beginning. Jerrod was young, very young, eight years old. How much of a sexual argument was in an eight-year-old? Did he still think as a baby or did certain disclosed fact or acts mean he's ready for a trial run? So that evening she came prepared to test Jerrod.

While she was reading to the young boy, she also purposefully let her bathrobe expose parts of her beautiful breast. She put the book down and asked Jerrod if he would like to touch her breast, as she was his mother, he need not be ashamed. So, she took his hand and put it on her breast. Never in his young life did he ever experience such a pleasure. He wanted more her perfume was intoxicating. So, when he thought enough was enough, she told Jerrod. She had to leave, so she left the poor lamb with his thoughts. Sandy figured that he was like any other male. Sandy was sure she had Jerrod hooked. Stay away a couple of nights, let the poor kid pine for her it worked as Jerrod asked the nurse to find out why Sandy did not see him for two nights. Instead the nurse told Sandy that she needs to give Jerrod some special medications and that Sandy did not have to read to Jerrod. Was the nurse suspicious? Not a good time to find out. Sandy called her attorneys and said that the boy was ready.

Judge Stein would be crucified. She told the attorneys to file the lawsuit and to get as much publicity that they could muster. Mr. Fong, Sandy's lead attorney was good. The papers were filed "Former Judge, Former husband was being sued by Sandy Froething for twenty-five million dollars and he was being accused of child molestation of an autistic boy of eight, her son. He was a pervert. The press and all segments of the media, television, and radio all had a field day. Sandy's team was on the offensive. This was big time. Her revenge would be complete plus a pot of gold. The gods were being good to her. The Stein's were stunned it seems that Jerrod's nurse's intuition was right on. Chad's hands were tied right from the beginning as Sandy and her scheming ways have been preparing forever and here, he comes with a briefcase full of papers with no writing on them. So, the jury was selected. It was hard to find impartial jury members because not many people had love for child molesters let alone a young boy afflicted with autism. Mr. Fong told Sandy that the Stein's were sentimentalist that because the hero that apparently saved Mr. Stein and happened to be an attorney albeit a rather small attorney was going to challenge him.

Mr. Fong was in court most of his adult life, defending multi giants of business, corporations so large that it was hard to conceive. They loved Mr. Fong because he was a winner. Whereas Chad Beecham shied away from court cases because they consumed too much of his time. He would have to neglect his clients to take on some more lucrative clients that needed court appearances. So, Mr. Fong proceeded he had Jerrod, who was now nine years old on the stand. Mr. Fong used his legendary experience to put Jerrod at ease. He told Jerrod who he was and would like to ask Jerrod a few questions. Just answer the questions truthfully. Before Mr. Fong could ask Jerrod any questions, he burst out crying. Jerrod was overly distraught that he was having difficulty breathing. His nurse Maya Cummins rushed to his aid, she had a respirator at the ready and she calmed Jerrod down. The Judge was a very perceptive man and he put two and two together. Mr. Fong was very large, with a bald head and a walrus mustache and a demeanor that was not child enhancing. So, the Judge ordered a ten-minute recess. Mr. Fong was furious, when he went back to the table, he told Sandy that's why I don't take cases like this. When the time was up and the court resumed, Mr. Fong was still agitated and his voice was full of anger. The Judge asked Mr. Fong to come to his elevated desk. He admonished Mr. Fong and told him the child was only nine years old and sickly on top of it, so get your act together. The Judge dismissed Mr. Fong and his gavel signified that court was resuming. Mr. Fong wasted no time and he said to Jerrod "Do you remember that I asked you if you knew right from wrong and you answered "Yes". The question is "Did former Judge Samuel Stein ever touch you? Jerrod answered "Yes" but before Jerrod could continue, Mr. Fong said you may step down. Judge I rest my case.

Jerrod was starting to get up from his seat but the Judge said for Jerrod to be seated as Mr. Beecham would like to ask you a few questions. Jerrod liked Chad Beecham and was at ease with him. Chad immediately said to Jerrod. "Jerrod you answered Mr. Fong's question only after your answer you were going to say more? Suddenly Mr. Fong slammed his fist down and said he objected to this line of inquiry. The Judge told Chad Beecham to stop that line of inquiry. Chad was now very upset but he answered the Judge with a very soft petulant yes. The Judge asked him to speak up as he did not hear him. So, Chad Beeham lost his cool and very loudly said yes. The Judge was very upset and he told Chad Beeham that he was imposing a fine of two-hundred-and fifty-dollars and another such outburst that he would he would be cooling off in jail. Now resume, but let me add after court write out a check and give it to the bailiff. Chad had to take a minute to gather his thoughts. Jerrod we all know that you know the difference between right and wrong, so I won't ask you again. Now Judge Stein would come to your room to read to you? Jerrod answered "I asked Judge Stein to read to me." Then you Jerrod. Now Jerrod, I am going to ask you to tell the Judge and jury you're meaning of touch. Take your time Jerrod.

So, Jerrod pondered a bit and then said to me there is good touch and bad touch. If the Judge or Maya brushed my hair down that would be a good touch. If the Judge kissed me on the check and said good night that would be a good touch. If someone gropes me by reaching into my pajamas that is real bad touch and Judge Stein never did that. Everything stood still for a few seconds, when all hell broke out. The jurist stood up and clapped. The gallery exploded clapping and yelling Jerrod's name. The sitting Judge was furious. He was pounding his gavel and shouting for the court to calm down. The bailiffs were trying their best to also restore order. When order was again restored the Judge said that the jury's actions and the gallery did the most unprecedented act that he has ever experienced and if there was another outburst, he would shut his court down. Bailiffs arrest anyone that is out of order. Now Mr. Beeham please proceed. So, Chad thanked Jerrod and told the Judge he rests his case. The Judge than instructed the jury and told them to retire to the jury room and try to reach a verdict. He then told the bailiffs that he would be in his chambers but to call him if the jury reached a verdict or had a question. Then he dismissed the court pending a verdict.

The wait wasn't very long and the bailiff told the Judge that a verdict has been reached. The Judge then asked the bailiff to instruct the lawyers to come at once. When both teams of lawyers were present the Judge asked the jury foreman if they had reached a verdict. The foreman stated "Yes" and were then instructed to read the verdict which was "This jury finds former Judge Samuel Stein "not guilty" of any of the counts and he handed the note to that effect to the bailiff to give it to the Judge. The Judge read to note that was signed by the Foreman and the other jurist and told the court that he would have a decision as to monetary compensation if any at tomorrow's session. Court dismissed at that bedlam again was rampant. Photographers trying to take pictures. News hacks trying to contact their firms. The earliest papers and viewing on television we're all pretty much on line with nine-year-old autistic boy fells giant Mr. Fong. Samuel Stein not guilty etc. One camp was devastated another camp was ecstatic. Chad Beeham came thru for the Stein's once again. Attorney Chad Beeham is the hero again. Chad and Madeline and the two Stein's were hugging and well acting like adolescents. Carl than told Donald that what happened is a prelude to what did happen and could happen and how certain events affect other events such as outcomes of governorship or even presidencies. The next day court was reconvened and the jury was there as well as the lawyers. So, the Judge told the court what his decisions were. First, he said former Judge Samuel Stein was found not guilty of all counts and it shall be noted as such to all departments in the government as to that effect.

Mrs. Sandy Frothing shall pay to Mr. Stein, twenty-five million dollars plus Mrs. Frothing will pay all the court fees and attorney fees. Mrs. Frothing has thirty days to comply with this order unless she can reach an acceptable agreement with Judge Stein and his attorney, Mr. Beecham, court is adjourned. Now that the Stein's could successfully count all the hatched chicks, Issac Stein said he would have a big victory party. The party that ensued was by far the biggest social event of the year. Hundreds were sent invitations. The guest of honor was Jerrod Da Vargas who was presented with the twenty-five-million-dollar check that Judge Stein received from Mr. Fong and Sandy. Jerrod said he would give the check to benefit

Autistic people all over the world. With that act many people all over the world sent Jerrod checks for his cause. Chad threw in a bombshell of his own when he announced that he and Madeline were to be married and Issac Stein agreed to be the best man.

When if and ever were things going to calm down as far as the mighty Mr. Bizzar was concerned the answer was never. And he proceeded to make his answer good as we are not finished with Mr. Bizzar and his actions. There were no more upheavals to be concerned with and life went its merry way. The one big event, after the victorious victory party that was held was the marriage of Chad and Madeline. The two were still madly in love and that probably would never change. In fact, their relationship never had ups or downs due to their personalities or habits if anything it was scary because it never is that smooth, but they seemed to have a knack of heading off a disagreement or any other adverse event as being trivial and not worth their effort. The marriage party was another big effort by Mr. Stein and son. It was mostly families and friends, but lurking in the shadows was Mr. Bizzar and some overtures of politics as there were far too many politicians and bankers present.

What happened was that Isaac Stein got an earful of a possible unexpected resignation of the now seated governor. The reason being diagnosed with liver cancer. It was not common knowledge but Governor Harris did let it slip out as to his future motives and Isaac Stein being a prominent member of the Wyoming Democratic Party got wind of it by just being Issac Stein.

Now Judge Stein and Issac Stein were always in tuned to the happenings of the party so the gears were meshing and they all pointed to Chad Beeham, but it was too early as no announcement was made by Governor Harris. Getting back to the wedding the

Stein's wedding gift to Chad and Madeline was very similar to what Judge Stein and Sandy received only this time it was not presented with a question mark. It was a legally split off portion of land quite close to Judge Stein's personal property. It was twenty-five acres encompassed by a six-foot wrought iron fence. The site was surveyed and the architect and surveyors agreed the perfect setting of a five thousand square foot home plus a small guest cottage adjourning the main house was a large patio paved with national stones or pavers from San Francisco streets, also adjourning the house and patio was a large swimming pool, parts of the pools apron was covered so that anyone seeking shade could sit or lie on elaborate pool furniture.

About one hundred yards from the pool was a tennis court with its own accompanying building that had showers, toilet arrangements and such. Isaac liked to play bocchi ball so he had an expert designer set up a good bocche ball court. So, all in all it was a beautiful elaborate gift to the couple. If money was offered it would have been refused. When the gift was presented to Chad and Madeline it was in the form of blue prints and a zillion sketches as the actual construction was not as yet started because Issac and the Judge wanted Chad and Madeline involved with their own personal choices. Two things happened to spoil the revere. One was devastating to Judge Samuel Stein. First the Judge was not available to receive a call from Governor Harris of Colorado, but Isaac the father took the call.

The Governor and Isaac were very good friends as Isaac being so prominent as a Democratic party leader sponsored Governor Harris as the choice for the Governor's seat at the last election. So, Governor Harris told Isaac that Sandy Frothing was dead. The groundskeeper for the Frothing estate discovered her body in the family pool. She drowned. The coroner's office staff is there now to retrieve the body and perform an autopsy. Sorry Isaac that I had to be the one to relay the sad news. I'm sure your son will be devastated. I'll hang up now so you can confront Samuel with the news and formulate your plans. The Judge was attending a rodeo in Bismarck, Wyoming. One of the cowboys at the Stein sheep ranch was a participant so the Judge and some of the other employees were going to attend and cheer their fellow employee to victory. Hopefully, as everyone figured when Judge Stein heard the news he couldn't conceive or grasps the news as being reality.

His mind went blank and his body was on the verge of collapsing. He took a sedative and it seemed to calm him down. His heart beat was so rapid that the doctor was in attendance and was afraid of a heart attack. It relieved him very much to hear that his father was on the way. Isaac figured that his son would want to go to Denver so Isaac instructed his secretary to arrange for passage for two and to keep him posted as to the flight time, and also set-up a suite with the favorite inn they always used in Denver. The secretary was very efficient and foresaw every need before they could be translated. The other event was that the governor of Wyoming was resigning due to poor health and Judge Stein and Isaac convinced the head party members to let Chad be their choice. Chad and Madeline agreed to the fact, so the small-time attorney from Cheyenne with no political experience was going to challenge a very prominent republican that was very experienced and very well liked.

Chad faced adversity a good part of his life, so where he was deficient in some respects, he made up for them by being honest and a tireless pursuant to the task on hand. Chad showed the world that he could handle himself when he beat the best top attorneys in the corporate world. There you have it. Disaster on one hand and a glimpse of the future on the other hand. Getting back to Sandy, the recorded facts were accidental drowning as there was no evidence of murder. She had a massive heart attack and succumbed to dying as a result. Isaac and his son would remain in Denver and attended the funeral. It's been two days now and the Judge is a waling ghost of what he once was. Regardless of the catastrophic recent events and how he was portrayed as the devil he loved Sandy and his fantasy she loved him. With hearts of lead they flew back to Cheyenne.

Isaac's personal secretary hired a chauffeured limousine to pick up the Judge and his father. They were home about three days when the Judge got a call from Helmut Gardener, Sandys and her deceased parents estate attorney. After a brief greeting, Mr. Gardener said that Sandy left an envelope for him to open, only upon her death or a legal posting of her lack of mental capacities to make decisions. Mr. Gardener asked if and when the Judge could come to his office as the documents had to be presented to the Judge personally. The appointment was made and they hung up. Two days later Judge Stein walked into Mr. Gardener's office which was located in one of the old established business sections of Denver. After a brief meeting and condolences, the two got to the task at hand. Attorney Gardener removed a large manila envelope that was bulging with documents. On the outside of the letter it was dated and said for Mr. Gardener to open the envelope only upon her death or mental lack of mental capacities. Then he checked a square that read Sandy Frothing deceased. He opened the envelope there was a rather large envelope marked only by the number one and there was a smaller envelope marked number two. Mr. Gardener read the cover letter to himself and Judge Stein. The first paragraph read Mr. Gardener the documents in parcel number one are legal papers signifying that I have deeded the twenty-five acres known as Frothing estate to my former husband, Judge Samuel Stein. There are also deeds to all the buildings, vehicles and machinery necessary to maintain Frothing Estate. Once the papers are signed, Samuel may dispose or keep the deeded properties and equipment. Paragraph two simply said the department store building located in downtown Denver address follows is also deeded to Samuel Stein. Paragraph three said that conclude the matters in envelope one. The cover letter goes on to say that envelope number two is personal and is to be handed to Samuel Stein unopened. If in the event Mr. Samuel Stein is deceased or mentally incapacitated envelope number two shall be shredded by a licensed firm and witnessed by two disassociate people from either your firm Helmut Gardener estate attorneys or any of Samuel Stein's associates within his enterprises. Thanks, Sandy. The envelope was then handed to Judge Samuel Stein.

The business was over and Judge Stein left. Mr. Gardener said that he would record all the deeds and send them to his office. Samuel Stein took a cab to the same I that his father and he occupied a few days ago. The Judge sat at a small leather topped desk and got out the personal letter from Sandy. His hands were shaking so bad that he had to take a sedative before he could comfortably continue. The letter read "My dear Samuel" I had to write this letter to you as the events of the latter period of my life did not ever change my love and feelings for you. I was an heiress so you knew I did not marry you for money but for love and respect. All through our married life excluding those two terrible incidents, we loved each other mutually. At the time of the first incident, I was possessed by an inner demon that controlled me totally. I visited with many doctors and psychiatrists which I hid from you because I did not want you to think I was mentally impaired. It was a mistake but I had no control the inner voice ran me much as we ran the toys we received when we were kids.

It sounds farfetched but my doctors told me there were many such cases and they believed what was happening and as sad as it was, they could only prescribe pills and sedatives to somewhat relieve the agony. The doctors wanted me to bring you to the sessions of therapy, but the inner voice said no, no way. As I write this, I realize that a strong person might have changed the scenario. It's been two years since the second encounter and I have not heard one word from the inner voices. Apparently, they gave up but I asked the doctors, what was their motives? They shrugged and excused themselves for not having answers as they were learning about mental distresses as well as the patients who were afflicted with them. The only bright spot in my case was the reprieve I was having whether it was temporary or a pause only time would tell. Also, the deeds signed over to you were not conciliatory actions because of my conscience but were always part of any plan to deed the properties to you as you were the only one that would do the right thing in case of my death.

This letter is for you, but if you want to make it public it's your choice. Love you always, Sandy. Tears of anguish came to Judge Stein. It could have been different and he loved her so much it was very gratifying to learn from her in her own words that she loved him even though the two court cases declared a different story. When the Judge got home, he showed his father the packet of signed over deeds plus her personal letter. The father always thought Sandy was a conniving woman with malice in her heart. Could he have been so wrong? In his cold assessment did he do a terrible injustice to the only person on earth he truly loved? Father and son were close, but is it true that close only matters in horseshoe play? Sandy is gone and my son is only an image of what he was just a few years ago. It's hard to fathom that Isaac with all his money and success. He let his son down. He would have to live with that for the rest of his life because there is no conveyable way to right such a wrong. By showing me the letter, was my son trying to tell me that all he really wanted was for me to love his wife as much as I loved him. Could I also have misJudged my son as much as I misJudged his wife? Simply because it was never mentioned, but apparently obvious because others mentioned to him. Educated beyond description, filthy rich but he could not see that two people wanted his love above everything else. The Judge picked up the envelopes and told his father to put them on the desk in the dining room as they should discuss what should be done with the deeds that would satisfy Sandy.

The Judge excused himself and said he had previous obligations for this evening and would the father convey that to Chad and Madeline who were coming to dinner. Imo was Mr. Stein's personal cook. She was of orient descent, very round and short. She thought she was Japanese but also something else and she assumed English because she loved fish and chips. If she loved spaghetti and meatballs, I guess that would have been part of her nationality but the fact was she loved Italian food. Isaac often remarked how Imo served up better Mexican, Italian and English prime rib. On she could cook and tonight it would be leg of lamb just the right amount of garlic and rosemary as lamb is delicate with mashed potatoes and gravy, plus a vegetable. You always left the table stuffed but always in ecstasy. Mr. Chad how about some vanilla ice cream and cherry pie? Imo was not going to let you off the hook until you were so stuffed you had to beg off. The next day, Samuel Stein arrived at his father's house. Imo immediately poured him some coffee and laid out a plate of cookies. So, father and son looked at the envelopes, but were reluctant to pick them up. Once they did, they were committed. The Judge could just say the inheritance was for me and let it go at that, but Judge Stein was adamant, he wanted Sandy indirectly through him to have her legacy that was due her. Mr. Stein and the Judge tossed around some possibilities, but they were all rejected. Mr. Stein suggested that the Frothing Estate be developed as a tribute to Autism awareness and therapy. The main house would be the headquarters. It was a two-story building, plus a basement in reality it was three stories to be developed.

Mr. Stein was getting excited as to whenever he was planning something he jumped in body and soul. Mr. Stein envisioned the completely remodeled basement as a laboratory to further study what was yet a mysterious illness. The ground floor would be the reception area for staff such as secretaries plus there would be larger and smaller offices devoted to executives. Some offices would be reserved for doctor patient consulting. The second story could be used for inpatient rooms. Judge Stein liked the idea and the two agreed that the miniscule details would be left to more knowledgeable persons such as architects, designers and engineers working hand in hand with the staff familiar to the needs of those afflicted with autism. Some buildings on the property would be raised others remodeled to meet a specific need. All in all, it could work and eventually be the main Autistic Center in America. The money, stocks and bonds in the Frothing living trust would be parceled out to the headquarters as needed. It was also brought out that some similar diseases could be incorporated under one roof. Carl than told Donald that the doctors detected a sign of pneumonia and ordered Carl to enter the hospital for a few days to get more comprehensive evaluation. Donald's father was going to visit for two days arriving tomorrow. In the meantime, you can go to town and see what you can gather regarding the elections. I gave you my opinion on who would be the front runners, you might check around and verify my choices.

The next day, my father arrived and we went directly to the hospital. My father talked to Carl's doctor who said it was a bad lingering cold or virus that sometimes turned ugly if not treated properly. Other than that, all his tests proved to be constant and Carl could be released tomorrow and to contact him to arrange it. The next day my father and I went to have Carl discharged from the hospital and to take him home. As I was driving to the hospital, I told my father that my head was bursting with Carl's speech. My father laughed and said if only the world had more Carl's in it! Events settled down or were they just getting ready to gather up steam again. Governor Harris made a formal announcement of his resignation and that it was Lieutenant Governor Herman Gardner the second in charge of Wyoming was made Acting Governor until a special election could be held, but now acting Governor Mr. Gardner was not happy. He had served two tines as Lt. Governor under Governor Harris. Mr. Gardner knew the political game top to bottom, but the Democratic Committee was going to sponsor Chad Beecham as the Governor. Mr. Gardner said that would be a death wish. "Imagine this "Snotty nosed kid" trying to invade his kingdom?" It was inconceivable what they were proposing. Their logic was a fresher more modern approach to a faster moving world. Old times have to step back a little so Wyoming can step forward. In a sense they were right. Wyoming was always ranching and open spaces. They had to modernize but their chances of achieving that goal was through him and not that snot nosed as head a better chance of winning the Governorship against the popular experienced Republican choice than did the inexperienced political novice Chad Beeham. The opposite camp was in ecstasy this was all falling into their laps without them exerting a word. The two top Democratic choices in discord would only help him. One small fly in the soup was that Chad was not playing along with Mr. Gardner's slandering. So, the Democratic Party tended to put a damper on Mr. Gardner's verbal assault as they didn't want the other party to come in through the back door and proclaim victory.

Two explosive events happened in succession. First, Governor Green passed away unrepentantly when he succumbed his illness was no better, nor worse so it was a shock. The second, Chad Beeham won the election and was now the Governor. It just proved the ups and downs of the political world, could never by predicated. So, chad and Madeline if nothing else presented Wyoming with a beautiful couple devoted to powering their State to greatness through honesty and integrity. Chad whispered into Madeline's ear "after the bedlam is over let's get some calamari fritter". There it was that quite musical giggle that he could never get enough of. Chad's life was turned upside down so many times now that Chad had to just go along with the flow. His one constant was Madeline and he loved her more than life itself and nothing else really mattered. Chad was a big achiever even in his younger days as a novice lawyer he never assumed that what he achieves someone else could do the same. So, he went about his duties as Governor of Wyoming full bent on succeeding but not for himself but for Wyoming. His work ethics and his honesty were part of him. Larger corporations trusted him and he in turn would not let them down. He brought prosperity to Wyoming by convincing the major railroads to lay networks of rails so that companies large and small could shop their product and compete, it was an even playing field so the firms using the rails made money the railroads made money so all in all prosperity was presented to Wyoming and new Wyoming was not just open land and ranches but a well-diversified state well equipped to challenge and win.

Chad's tenure as Governor is almost in its first year and already the issue of what's next us cropping up, but for had its one day at a time, that's what makes him tick. He naturally thinks ahead, but his biggest bet is today. So everyday some media guy or promoter of sorts asks him what's net as if its tomorrow, when he still has over a year to go in his Governorship. So, Chad tells them it's too early and it hasn't crossed my mind yet. So, they go back to their papers or offices and try to answer the questions themselves. So, they begin Governor Chad Beecham has little time to get a plan of action in place. He could run for Governor again, because he did do a heck of a job his first term. He could elect to run for a Senate seat or house seat. President Groom is going to take a run at a second term and rumor has it that his Vice President won't be invited back. Chad could conceivably be President Groom's next Vice President. Chad is young, he could just elect to set it all out and be as advance publicist for himself by visiting sitting Governor's and political figures and just be the face of politics because President Groom can only do this last quest for the presidency coming up, than the law says he is out, but if Chad works his magic, President Groom could endorse him and President Groom is so popular that it could not hurt, not in the least. The "Snot nosed kid" has so many options that he might just throw a dart because most of his options are meaningful. So, Donald told Carl, I wasn't around than, but there were rumors of President Groom selecting a different Vice President. Was that just a rumor? How did it play as you and my dad covered the election? So, Carl was pleased that Donald encouraged this line of thought as Mr. Bizzar loomed big in the Presidents second term. I'll tell you Donald, politics will never be the same. It all began towards the end of President Groom's first term and towards the end of his second term. So, here is how it went down. Chad was into the second year of his first term and already the political gears were starting to mesh. Both parties were starting to evaluate potential players. The same scenario was taking place regarding the next Presidential race albeit it was still over a year before it came into focus. Carl still said it seems that hardly has the President elect received his oath to the office than they are off and running talking about the next election although its four years early. Modern day politics is a merry-go-round that never stops. But since there is such a large framework in time, hundreds of potential presidential devotees are weighed and most are chewed a bit and spit out. Some last longer but in the end it's just two or three that strike gold and eventually one president emerges.

So, the planning goes on, not only for President by for Vice President, Secretary of State on and on and President Groom was no different. He wanted all his ducks lined up so that he and the American public could see the direction the wind was blowing. Not only President Groom, but also his political foes were all positioning themselves which leads us to the informal dinner invitations presented to Chad and Madeline by President Groom and his wife, Phoenix. Phoenix told Chad and Madeline it was not a state dinner where ties and tails were the norm, but this was informal come as you are. Chad and Madeline presented themselves at the appointed time. Naturally there is nothing that goes down in Washington that it doesn't have to be let alone. Big events or little events it's all the same. Media political parties, television you name it and they are all trying to find out why the Wyoming Governor and his wife are having dinner with the President in Washington, D.C. At any given time, there are hundreds of men and women in the political and society arena from all over the world vying against each other to just get one event right that might escalate them up the ladder of success. They all its competitiveness but really its dog eat dog, no mercy is shown, your best friends are for the time being just another of the hungry other hundreds all aiming for the same goal. So, the Presidents Press Secretary interviews and tries to assure the attendees at the meeting that it's nothing more than a friendly get to know you type of dinner. The President has in the past had many such dinners. So, they are appeased, but not convinced. The president and his wife noticed that Chad and Madeline were not awed by the fact that they were in the presence of the President and his wife. It was like they frequently went to dinner at President's home as for that matter maybe kings and queens' courts. So, the President asked Chad if he was not a little curious as to why they were here. Chad thought about the question for a second and said you know Mr. President rumors were rampant that you were going to give me four or five cabinet posts and I was just wondering if I could handle that many. All four got a bang out of that and so far as President Groom was concerned the Governor was not going to be tripped up easily. So, while they were in the midst of dinner, the President said to Chad. "You know that I and my present Vice President do not seem to see things in the same light, so I told Admiral Hastings that he would not be my running mate for the next election, now that is not a rumor. So, I would like for you to be my Vice President." Chad and Madeline were dumb founded. The President continued on to say that the Democratic heads and I discussed this and were more than pleased. You and I would be given one hundred percent by the National Committee. Thank you, President Groom, but it did kind of came out of the blue. I would like to talk to my wife and could I possibly give you my answer shortly? The President agreed, but insisted that shortly be short as he said that his press secretary would have to arrange for national coverage announcing his intentions to drop the present Vice President and let the world know that his choice was Chad Beeham. Now Donald that's what I mean about politics and the bizarre events, but bizarre is not done by a long shot, I fact he's just beginning. So, Chad and Madeline went back to Wyoming. On the airplane Madeline said to Chad that she thought that Phoenix was really nice and she would like the opportunity to get better acquainted. Chad said is that a confirmation that I should accept the Vice President invitation, again that musical giggle. You know Madeline, without even addressing what this whole dinner was about I might as well get on the phone and tell the President "I'm your man" because Madeline likes Phoenix. Politics is strange indeed. So, Chad and Madeline were greeted by the inevitable news seeker. Don't they ever sleep? Judge Stein went to the airport to pick-up Chad and Madeline. Chad said to the Judge "thank goodness your father had the foresight to put that six-foot wrought iron fence around the perimeter of the lot or I would be worn out answering the doorbell. The Judge never was one to get to animated he was usually noncommittal but, in this case, he said "Chad it comes with the territory". Chad had a heck of a job trying to outfox the fox meaning the media. They were relentless, question after question. It would only end when President Grooms, Press Secretary would announce that the president would be on national T.V. with some important news. In fact, this event was happening tonight. So, the President always gracious and considerate addressed the American people by saying that Admiral George Hastings his current Vice President would not be his running mate in the coming election and he gave the podium over to the Admiral. He thanked the president and then told the world that due to personal reasons he would not be President Groom's running mate, but if things got better, he would not be averse to a cabinet post. It was short and to the point. The President than let the cat out of the bag. "My running mate would be Chad Beeham the present Governor of Wyoming. "It was bedlam, reporters running to telephones it seems that the story of Chad's life was bedlam and chaos, one thing after another. After the bombshell the President addressed some other matters and now Chad was in for a penny or a dollar.

Chad still had his present term as Governor to either resign now or fulfill his term. Chad elected to finish his term as the people of Wyoming would not be too happy that two governors' in a row did not finish their terms in office. Chad's Lt. Governor was a middle aged African American lady that knew politics backward and forward. Chad often said "I'm never stumped because I have Jessica Gomey at my side." Jessica is indispensable in a world that proclaims everyone is disposable. Jessica will be the next Governor of Wyoming if I have anything to say about that she has my complete support. My only regret is leaving Jessica behind, but Wyoming needs her so I will be fair to the Wyoming I love and say that I will not take her with me to Washington, D.C. Carl said to Donald that "Jessica was one in a million and he could go on about Jessica for a long time, but for now all I can say is we will all be hearing of Jessica Gomey in the future". Chad finished his term and there was still time before the presidential circus would start so he brainstormed unofficially, he visited in office governor, he visited senators and of course CEO's of big companies. He also found time to spend with Madeline, camping and fishing. Finally, the presidential race was on and President Groom won handily meaning that Chad Beeham was now the Vice President of the United States of America. In Chad's case it's like to roulette wheel where it stops nobody knows. Since the election everything quieted down to a normal pace. Naturally the thoughts among the big players were such as where do we go from here.

Most thought that with the Presidents walloping victory and the ascend of his new Vice President that a dynasty was in the making. Like any major function while in its infancy there is a lot of maneuvering, a lot of expended energy but it soon winds down to the same old, same old. In other words, business as usual. So, the President and Chad had plenty of time to reminisce and project different scenarios. One given was that President Groom was not legally qualified to run for office a third time. Two term period and this was his second term. So naturally the talk was about a successor that could keep the momentum moving. President Groom was barely into his second term when he was besieged with a barrage of questions as to whom would succeed him. He held up his hands and said. "Hey let me get my seat warm before you ship me out to pasture. Let's discuss this in a year or so. In the meantime, your media people find yourself some other topic to pursue. Political parties do not wait so they asked President Groom to feel out the best possible successors and give them some clue as to the direction they could choose. So, one day the President sent Chad a note saying tomorrow morning I would like your presence at about nine thirty a.m. for a little chat. I'll have coffee and cookies for us. Chad by this time knew the president quite well and he said to himself "a little chit chat, baloney, President Groom does not chit chat." Never the less Chad was in the President's office at 9:30 a.m. because the President loved his sweets so that was always a sure thing, the sweets would be good and predictable the little chit chat not so but it sure would not be the price of fish in today's markets. The coffee and cookies and pastries were excellent as expected. Why couldn't he just say come over and have some coffee instead of this little chit chat business that gets your stomach rolling so that you can't even enjoy your coffee and cookies.

    President Groom's chit chats could be starting a war with some nation or just be about attending a birthday party for some Governor's daughter, in other words unpredictable as to why he has called. The president began to say "As you know Chad, I am not eligible to run for office as my two terms will be up." There was a long pause as he ate another cookie and then remarked about how good it was, he then proceeded to say "My good friend Jay as the head of our political party wants me to feel you out about being my successor, there you have it." That is what I had expected a nice solar plexus right hand punch. No warning just wham! Chad should be used to these punches as he had experienced a few good ones in the past. Once again Chad was speechless. The president liked it when he overwhelms someone so he held up his hands and said "I know you want time to talk it over with Madeline and laughed. So, Chad cleared his throat and gave a little laugh and said "You know how it is President Groom." The little chit chat was over.

    Madeline and Phoenix hit it off very well and they really liked each other. I guess it might have been a mother daughter relationship as Madeline had lost her mother when she was still young and missed her very much. Phoenix on the other hand, never knew her mother nor had she ever had any sisters or for that matter a daughter to love. When Phoenix learned that Madeline was the former owner of Madeline's Boutique she was thrilled as she used to trade their whoever she visited relatives in Cheyenne where she was born. So, it was natural for Phoenix and Madeline to visit every boutique in Washington, D.C. The only problem was the public, at first it was flattering but that soon wore off, also everywhere they went a secret service shadow loomed tall, woe and more woe to the secret service agent that was guilty of these two precious people being demeaned in any way. Chad and Madeline decided to not run for the Presidency. It was a decision of two people so much in love that they wanted to be selfish and enjoy each other while the opportunity was still there. So, the following day, Vice President, Chad Beecham told President Groom of his intentions. President Groom was very gracious and told Chad that he would inform the officers of the National Committee his decision to not be a part of the next election.

It was an easy decision for Chad, but it was hard to convey his message to President Groom, but it got done. The subject was not brought up again after it was conveyed to the President, but unbeknown to Chad the President told his wife, Phoenix, that he admired a person that stood up for his convictions. So, one day let into another and the President told Chad that the powers at the National center wanted to be sure that Chad had not changed his mind and if the President would be as kind as to ask Chad if there was any change. Chad and President Groom were in the President's office when Chad was asking the question "Are you sure?" Chad answered, "Yes that he and Madeline were adamant and would not seek the Presidency." At that point, President Groom walked over to the two men seated in the shadows and said "There you are gentlemen directly from Chad". The two nodded to Chad and the President and left. It was a formality that had to take place before President Groom would make it public on National T.V. that they were eliminating any chance of error by having their two lawyers hear it said by Chad. Time went by but there were no major issues and legislation was brought forward and discussed. Some Senate hearings were brought up all in all the whole Senate and house could have used their time better by going fishing, but what was really happening was that the presidential opponents were at it. Debates and other sorts of political fare were takin place as the jockeying for position by both parties was becoming more evident.

The Republican Party was moving ahead very fast towards their goal of selecting the best choice for the presidency. Eliminations were taking place as fast of the process. When the time comes for any type of office such as Governor or Presidency, many people want to try their hand at maybe becoming the people's choice. Most early entries strike out early because of various reasons, manly money and backing by some political faction. Regardless of why the field becomes thinner and thinner as the time for a major runner up approaches. In this case it happens that Arthur Sorenson the Governor of New Mexico is the people's choice so far. He has accumulated enough voted that he will be the Republican choice. The national convention always a big part of the political process will put on a big show or formality and nominate Arthur Sorenson as their guy.

The Democratic process is similarly and the convention will take place within the next two months. The front runner there is Sarah Westbrook a Senator out of Rhode Island. Sarah Westbrook is very qualified and her an Arthur Sorenson both present about the same amount of experience and are both very well liked. Both party representatives lack in the field of foreign relations and in this day and age it is a must to push yourself forward, but in this case they both lack a lot of foreign experience so it's not quite as if one excelled at the foreign level and could hold it over the other. Once the two conventions are over their choices cemented in a calm set in and then the two choices by their representatives' parties make a big push to gain favor by the whole U.S. population and therefor win the presidency. President Groom and Vice President, Chad Beeham throw in their position although they both are not part of the actual function. So, they have more or less been looking in from the outside and going about their business of being President and Vice President. So, they contrive to occasionally devote some time to some personal enjoyment. In the case of President Groom, it's a little round of golf as that is his passion. So, his set-up a date with Vice President Chad to play some golf. Two Senators happened to be in in town and they both were avid golfers, so the President included them to play that day, also they used the game to pick each other's brain in regard to the pulse of the population in their State and any other choice gossip as politicians are ripe to any and all types of gossip. "Now Donald" Carl said "We are going to see Mr. Bizzar at work to try and throw a monkey wrench into the whole show and convince everyone of his powers to mold situation to his liking."

The foursome was going to play at the prestigious Country Club golf course. The country club was an exclusive membership club. Very expensive, very exclusive. The only way for a nonmember to become a member is a very drawn out process. Money is only a factor. A nonmember has to submit a profile of his life he has to be represented or sponsored by an existing member that the whole package is reviewed by the membership committee. The nonmember is also presented to the committee in person and he is asked questions such as why he wants to be a member. What his political leanings are, about his religious affairs and many sexual questions and comments. The club itself is huge, the main floor is a large, carpeted space with expensive chairs and couches and near the entrance is a large oval counter where the club president usually resides and greets members. There is a very elaborate telephone system with operators working twenty-four hours a day to accommodate members. The main floor also has a separate large room that is a four-star equivalent restaurant. Members and their family are the only people that the restaurant administers to. The public is not admitted unless they are a guest of a member. The second floor is only accessible by elevator. It covers the whole footprint of the club itself. Part of the room is carpeted and many seating arrangements are throughout. Along the wall is a huge bar that is manned by professional bartenders. Along another wall is a segregated area with leather top desks for members to write letters or do office work for their own personal use. A long wall separates the lounging area and that room is a gamming room for members to play cards and other games. No actual cash is visible everything from drinks to sandwiches is on a signed tab only. The tab has to be cleared each month with no exceptions to this rule. The grounds area has an eighteen whole golf course, many tennis courts, covered and not covered, swimming pools with extensive aprons for tables and chairs with umbrellas for shade all to be used by the members. One area of the property is devoted to housing where about twenty-five single family homes are scattered on plots of one acre to five acres this whole area is a locked gated community and is only available to members that want to reside near the club house. There are too man amenities for members use to go into detail. A few of the more popular are a separate building which all buildings use the general format of the club house. This particular building houses spas and tanning rooms with massage tables and certified masseuses. Another such buildings are a weight room with all types of exercise equipment also manned by professional athletic instructors. The most popular and most used is the golf course and to keep it functioning properly reservations have to be made. Cancellations are permitted, but notice has to be given so that the space can be reserved.

Any time the president reserves the golf course it is immediately cordoned off to all members. There are four secret service police that attends to the course at that time where the president is there. Their first task is to walk the eighteen holes and warn people that they are off limits while the president is playing, also they try to pick out various areas that might be strategic to an assassination attempt or attack. The three people with the president this day are Vice President Chad Beeham and two Senators. The secret service police or agents are positioned as such. Ty Wilson on one side he was the senior agent in charge. On the other side was agent Justin Pratt. To the rear was agent Jim Sommerfield and the front was agent Jackson DuPree. After each hole is played the foursome have to wait for Jackson DuPree to walk the course to the next hole so he okayed if everything is a go to play the hole. At the fourth hole they are interrupted by two telephone calls. Ty Wilson is the agent the calls are put through to. Madeline Beeham would like to talk to her husband. Madeline told Chad she was not feeling well and was going to visit her doctor. Chad got nervous and he said that he would rush home and take her to the doctor. Madeline insisted that he keep playing and that Phoenix, the President's wife would drive her to the doctor's office and that she would call when her visit was over. "In the meantime, dear husband breaks a leg."

The second telephone call that came was for Senator Barry Johnston and it was that Mr. Johnston had an important certified letter waiting for him by his assistant at the club house desk. They had two golf carts available for their use and Senator Johnston said he would drive the cart to retrieve his letter. So, while he was gone, they hung around and waited for his return. So, everyone relaxed a bit. The President Chad and Senator Howard Blink engaged in political talk. The secret service agents were relaxed but stayed at their positions. Just then a brand-new maintenance truck appeared out of nowhere and was driving very fast toward hole number four.

Ty Wilson was aghast and he ran towards the truck waving his arms and commanding it to stop. It kept coming forward. Ty Wilson recognized the driver as James Harden and he yelled for James to turn around and go back to the club house. James Harden stopped the truck and got out of the truck before Ty Wilson could command him to get back in. James Harden had a machine pistol armed at Ty Wilson but it did not fire it malfunctioned so Ty Wilson killed James Harden. The person seated in the jump seat behind the driver Patrick Sosen fired and killed Ty Wilson. The back agent, Jerry Sommerfield ran to assist Ty Wilson but was gunned down by Patrick Sosen but before he died, he managed to shoot and kill Patrick Sosen. The front passenger shooter was Marcel Handy he had a clear view of the gofers, He shot seven times at President Groom and killed him instantly. He shot at Senator Howard Black four times and killed him instantly. Marcel Handy than opened fire at Chad Beeham but Chad was a short distance away from the President and Senator Black. So, Marcel Handy had to readjust his shooting position. He shot and hit Chad's right arm and hand shattering it with four shots. The lead agent Jackson DuPree was shooting at the passenger shooter Marcel Handy so Marcel had to take cover or be killed. Marcel got along side of the front-end passenger side and started shooting at Jackson DuPree but his shots were ineffective. Before Marcel could get in position to shoot at Jackson DuPree, he himself was shot in the shoulder by Agent Justin Pratt but Justin Pratt must have taken some hits when the shooter Marcel was firing at the President because he was found dead near the President. All this action took place in less than five minutes. Sirens were blasting away; ambulance and police were speeding towards whole number four. Marcel Handy was injured but not dead so he took a vial out of his pocket and swallowed two cyanide pills and he died instantly by taking the pills and he knew he could not be interrogated if he was dead. The other Senator was being brought back to hole number four by one of the club employees. They got about half way there when the shooting started so the driver turned to head back to the club house when the shooter behind the passenger Amos Sterling opened fire at the jeep and he killed Senator Barry Johnston and the driver of the jeep kept on going as the weight of the employees foot accelerate the jeep that finally stopped when it hit a parked car.

After Amos Sterling shot and killed the jeep driver and the Senator, he too took out a vial with two pills and swallowed them and he died instantly. Meanwhile Jackson DuPree scrambled to the side of Chad Beeham and could see the President and the Senator were both dead so he administered to Chad. At first Jackson DuPree though the Vice President was also dead but all the blood was coming from his shattered arm. He immediately removed his tie and made a makeshift tourniquet that he tightened with his pistol until the bleeding was virtually stopped. The first ambulance arrived and Jackson motioned them over to Chad. The medics were good, they immediately stopped the bleeding with a professional tourniquet. One of the medics set up a portable blood transfusion and another ambulance showed up and they set up a portable unit that registered Chad's vital signs. An ambulance helicopter landed close by and Chad was put on a gurney and loaded into the helicopter than they took him to the hospital. The doctors were waiting and the operating team was in place. There was no hope for the arm it was shattered by all the hits it took and they had to amputate the arm to save Chad's life. His life was already saved by the heroics and quick thinking of agent Jackson DuPree.

The world was stunned. It seemed that all the gears stopped turning and the world stopped and everyone was whispering. Now would the Vice President make it? His vital signs were low but steady and Chad lost a lot of blood and his life was in the hands of faith. Slowly but surely, minute by minute he seemed to be rallying back. If he pulled through this, the big thing would be the lack of blood to the brain, but his vital statistics seemed to indicate that the problem might have been nipped in the bud by the fast actions of Jackson DuPree and the ambulance crew. At the scene of the shooting all the dead bodies lay as they were. Special teams had to be brought in by the F.B.I. every bullet had to be found and recorded, every blade of brass with blood had to be marked. It was going to be one investigation by the F.B.I.

Mr. Bizzar was pleased but he still had work to do. Phoenix was sent home from the hospital after Madeline's doctor said they would keep her overnight for further examinations, while she was home, she got news of her husband being killed. Phoenix fainted and the friends opted to take her to the emergency room of the hospital which was about four blocks away. When they arrived at the hospital, she was dead on arrival, she just stopped breathing. Phoenix was not young anymore and she had some issues but they all were being treated and nothing showed signs of disaster. She had asthma and was also being treated for a heart problem. Her last visit the doctors told her that everything was steady and to pursue a normal life. The American population was stunned. When would the carnage stop? So many dead in just under five minutes.

It was hard to believe the four shooters seemed to be working independently. They naturally knew each other as they worked together as a team for many years. They did not know each other. There was never any mention of any kind of a plot by any of the men. There was no social contact with each other except at work. Not once did one of the shooters and his family ever attend a social gathering with each other. The wives of the four shooters did not really know each other. The only connection that any of the shooters had in common was they all had a vial of two cyanide pills. Not one of the shooters had a gun at home and they were never seen at a shooting range. They were in total just the average family man, not one of these people ever had a reason to be contacted by police for domestic violence, drinking or any other vice that might have attracted notice. It was all conjecture but it was assumed by the F.B.I. that at the last moment one of the four had the guns and ammunition. One of the four instructed the others as to whom their targets were. Somehow each knew that the day of reckoning was here otherwise when they were told to shoot and kill there did not seem to be any questions or hesitation.

It was weird that four people working together for years never knew that this particular day was coming. All four-landscape people were investigated each year by the F.B.I. simply because they worked at the clubhouse and periodically very important people such as the President, Senators and top rank CEO's of large corporations all used the facilities at the private country club. Not one of the men had a black mark on their records. In fact, Mr. Wilson knew James Harden's father when James Harden father was the head of the landscape crew. When he retired over fifteen years ago, his son who worked with him was named senior landscape employee and became the boss man. In the course of Ty Wilson knowing the father and son for over twenty years there was never any reason for him to write up either man because their slates were clean.

The F.B.I. had special equipment that checked each inch of the walls for concealed space that could hide guns and ammunition or could possibly give some clue as to how this event happened. Each home was characterized as a normal home in a very normal neighborhood. The neighbors talked highly of the families of the shooters and they all seemed to attend neighbor by functions at the local school and churches. These must have been a fifth agent that had no association with the country club and this person was not known to the F.B.I. and he on this particular day brought to the landscape crew the guns and ammunition and cyanide vials. It was strange that if the shooters were not trained to use these particular firearms how they managed to work the weapons let along be proficient in the handling of the guns and hit their targets. The F.B.I. will be pondering this act for many years to come much like the President John F. Kennedy tragedy.

The surgeons had to amputate Chad's arm and put him on vital monitoring machines. Chad was heavily sedated but eventually he brought back to the world of living. Chad tried to move but was heavily restrained. Chad asked or Madeline but the doctors were reluctant to inform him that Madeline had expired as she had suffered an eruption to her brain that killed her instantly. It was diagnosed as the wall of the artery bursting and she literally drowned. Chad might have had a relapse if he was told so they held back the information about Madeline. Chad started to show immediate improvement which was very encouraging as the matter of the Presidency was paramount now that he was coming out of the anesthesia. A team of four doctors examined Chad, plus three prominent brain surgeons to determine if could handle mentally and physically to continue with the office of the presidency. All the physicians and surgeons agree that his vital signs were stable and that he could take the vows of the incoming President.

The world was informed that Chad Beeham would be stepping in as the new President of the United States of America as of ten o'clock a.m. the following day. Many dignitaries from all over the world were present to witness Chad Beeham take the oath of office and he was now President. President Chad Beeham was helped to standup at the podium and the piece of paper that he jotted some words on flew away. Someone retrieved the paper and handed it back to Chad. Chad looked at the piece of paper and said "I don't need this piece of paper to tell me how proud I am to be an American and proud to be your President." "I will be the best President that I can be. Thank you!" Chad sat down in the wheelchair and he was exhausted and he would now begin to serve the remainder of President Groom's term out. Carl told Donald that Chad would fulfill his duties as President in an admirable way than its up to the American people to vote Arthur Sorenson who was declared the choice for his party or Sarah Westrock who still had to be officially nominated by her part at the upcoming convention. So, Carl rightfully picked the two to represent their respective parties. Donald said that his father would bet all he owned on Carl's decision and his father laughed but I 'm not a betting man. Regardless my father was trying to tell me Carl was more right than wrong.

The convention would be held in Miami in seven days, but tragedy struck Sarah Westrock and she was now dead. The world would mourn another great American maybe the future President and the first woman President. It so happened that Bill Westrock and Sarah were having a bowl of clam chowder at an outside café. Someone tapped Bill's shoulder and excused himself and asked if he was Bill. Bill said "My name is Bill who are you?" The man answered that he was Captain Ricco which meant nothing to Bill Westrock until the man unraveled his story in broken English. He said that he was a captain of a twelve-seat deep sea fishing boat and Bill who was an avid fisherman caught a record sized marlin. A he talked he pulled out his wallet and showed Bill a photo of the captain and Bill proudly holding up the large fish. Then Bill remembered and shook Captain Ricco's hand and laughing told Ricco "Hey that was a long time ago let's see about five years ago." Ricco said "yes, you no change, I old now. So, Bill asked him what he did now and Ricco said that his boss have two boats. "We are busy, many people like fishing the big fish, but Marcel like money to much and he smuggle drugs". "He and his new captain are in jail for twenty years, money no good in prison. I save my money and buy small boat to seat five and am busy all the time."

Bill and Sarah decided that the convention was seven days off that they could enjoy a day at sea, so right then and there they booked themselves on Captain Ricco's next which was the next day. Bill and Sarah arrived at the pier and they were hailed by Captain Ricco. Three men were already seated at their stations so Bill and Sarah sat in the remaining two seats. It was five a.m. and Captain Ricco said it would be one hour before they could be in fishing waters, so he told everyone to relax and off they went. Coffee and pastries were served and the time passed quickly. Captain Ricco had one engineer that maintained the engines and setup the fishing seats. He appeared young but Ricco said he was the best. About 9:00 a.m. they entered the water and Ricco thought would bring forth a big bounty of fish. He said he always very lucky here. Suddenly there was a big flash and explosion and all five seats and occupants were blown into the ice-cold water.

Bill was killed instantly and Sarah was just barely alive holding onto a piece of debris. Of the three other fisherman, two were dead but one was also holding onto debris. Ricco's engineer was dead also. Ricco himself was in the cabin steering so he did not get the brunt of the explosion, but he was knocked unconscious and by the time he regained consciousness the oil and gas was ablaze around the boat. Captain Ricco phoned the Coast Guard and yelled May Day. The operator calmed Ricco down and got his bearings. The Coast Guard was at least eight minutes away. The passenger near Sarah was badly burned and Sarah was just out of reach of the fire. Eventually the man could not hold on any longer and he went underwater. Sarah was the only one alive at this point. The Captain could not escape from the boat as the fire was all around so he dove into the fire and figured he could get under it and swim to safety, but it did not work as he tried to surface and gulp air the flames were to hot and he went under.

The Coast Guard finally arrived and plucked Sarah out of the ice-cold water. Hyperthermia already set in on Sarah although the Coast Guard wrapper her in blanket. The Coast Guard boat made a valiant charge for shore but Sarah was unconscious by the time they reached shore and put her in an ambulance and she was gone. The Coast Guardsmen did not know who Sarah was as all I.D. was lost at sea, but when the ambulance arrived at the hospital someone recognized her as Sarah Westrock and from that moment on the media was in a frenzy trying to tie the story together. Sarah Westrock was on the verge of greatness of winning or losing her presidential bid and she had already attained a remarkable affinity with the American people. They just liked her and they trusted her so again the big loser was the American and the American people.

We as a nation has gone through adversity these last few months and have been mercilessly cruel so much happened. We did not need another great American to fall. In the wake of this latest tragedy the political party was in utterly a party of chaos. So close yet so far. It has never happened before that days, one short week could make such a profound impact upon the political scene. Both parties were affected. Arthur Sorenson was now faced with the unknown. Sarah was his opponent and Sarah he knew now that he faced an unknown face and possibly a great set-back to his momentum. Could the presidency be on hold? After all, even is Sarah's party had or has someone in the wings, seven days is not much time to put everything into perspective after all Arthur Sorenson and Sarah and other hopefuls have been campaigning for over two years.

Sarah's party was to hold an emergency meeting to find out what was to be done? President Beeham would also be there. Issac Stein and his son, Judge Samuel Stein both affluent party members would be present. The meeting would be a closed-door session to the media and other political activists. Guards were placed around the room. Special engineers with sophisticated instruments scanned every inch of the large room for bugs as small as a pin head that could be placed almost anywhere. In the past, bugs have been found in telephones, pictures hanging on the wall, a pen set on a desk even a bug implanted in the pen itself. Also, a sound proof wall was erected outside the room to prevent sound devices as far as one block away from getting in on the room. These listeners were very effective and seeing that they could be as close or as far as a block away hidden in a room or a rooftop. Foreign countries used these instruments to overhear meetings at prestigious places like the U.N., the Pentagon. So, to counter their effectiveness special rays were imposed on all the outside and roof of certain buildings when important meetings were taking place these special rays broke up the sound paths so in reality everything was gargled and ineffective. The meeting was effectively ordered to begin. There were two stenographers typing the whole meeting plus they recorded every word, much like the machines used in court cases.

The President of the National Party addressed the group and came right to the point. We are in need of a replacement for Sarah and not just anyone but someone that can win for us. So, I ask each and every one present to reach back and ponder a prospective person and we will with cautious judging consider each and every name presented. Issac Stein said that the only person that stood a chance was President had Beeham if he could be persuaded to accept the challenge, but he was adamant that he would retire after he served the remaining time from President Groom's term. Chad was non-committal he just listened and sipped his coffee. Other names were brought forth but it was evident that they all fell short. Person after person seconded Issac Stein as their choice, but the fact remained that it was President Chad's choice and he had no such thing in his vocabulary that he owed. Because all his years in public office he gave all he could. He still sat uncommitted. Issac Stein was a shrewd business man and at one time a very prominent lawyer and he had a feeling that this was not going as he anticipated, so he asked for a recess so he could talk to Chad personally. The recess was granted and Issac Stein asked President Chad Beeham if they could talk in private for a few minutes. Issacs and Chad were like father and son, but in this case Issac was cruel an unmercifully and unfair when he said to Chad. "Madeline would have said yes "and that's all he said. Tears were rolling down the faces of both then. Both loved each other and trusted each other. All Chad said was "I'll try my best and it was over." The vote was one-hundred percent in favor of choosing Chad. President Chad Beeham would represent their party and try to achieve what many though an impossible task. Now Chad was in and like so many of his trials and tribulations once he was in, he would be in for all his worth. The next day the Press Secretary announced that the President had an important message and would be on national television at five p.m. eastern time. Thank you!

So, he approached the podium and acknowledged all present. When I was at the podium after being sworn in as President of the United States. I had this little piece of paper with some choice words for me to glance at the wind caught it and accidently it sailed off. Today I have a similar piece of paper with no writing on it and this time no accident I know it to the wind. "Americans all will miss Ms. Sarah Westrock so I ask all of you to honor her with a moment of silence." Tears and hurt were all incorporated in that moment of silenced. When it was over the president said "secondly, I am going to announce now that I will be the presidential candidate for my party not to fill Sarah's shoes but to keep fill the void that was left." After the President left some announcer recapped the President's words. The President today has enlightened us as to some questions that the American people needed answered. Arthur Sorenson now knows who he will be facing for the next few months pending the vote for the President of the United States.

The American people now have the answer as to who will be Arthur Sorenson's and his party's challenger. The next four years ae going to be very challenging for the President elect come November. Both Chad Beeham and Arthur Sorenson were knowledgeable about foreign affairs and that should point whoever wins in the right direction. Both Arthur Sorenson and Sarah acknowledged that we had to build up our military and our anti-missiles program to cope with the unrest in the world that keeps chattering about I'm stronger than you and if you provoke me you will regret it. The reality is that there is a lot of unrest in the Middle East and also in Asia. With the Presidency will also come the job issues that seem to hand on to the tail coat of the incoming President. November was approaching fast. Both camps seemed to make in roads and both camps seemed to lost some. It actually was win some and lose some.

Arthur and Chad were very good political friends although they each represented the opposite views on many issues. Arthur had a big advantage over Chad in the fact that his campaigning was favorable and though his momentum slowed it still was formidable. Also, Chad never really had a chance to build up his depleted body after the shooting and the psychological effect that losing Madeline had. So, to many, Chad was not completely the strong challenger that he was in the past. Chad had some virtues that could not be ignored. He was well though of by both parties' constituents and he showed that favoritism was not a part of his act. While Vice President, he showed a remarkable admiration for many of his friends of both parties that brought forth good sustainable ideas. He believed in an America undivided and America that would come together in times of adversity. He also believed in education and said that that separated the haves from the have nots. So, to sum it all up they were both two friends in the ring to win, but when it was over, they would still be friends. The election came and to no one's mind, Chad Beeham won. Chad had just a little bit of advantage here and there that Arthur Sorenson could not match. Some would say the end result was close, other not so close. The end result was that Chad Beeham was the new and old President. He would take his oath and like always he would tell the American people that "I will be the best President I can be." Chad endured as much of his success as his body could endure and he went home to rest. The partying would go on and on but Chad had to excuse himself. Chad got ready to lose himself in sleep, but he sat on the edge of the bed and cried. Presently Madeline came and wiped the tears from his eyes and she said "Chad it's no sin for a grown man to cry" and she was gone.

Did this happen? He believed it did, but reality said it didn't, but he was glad he believed she came. He loved her so much. Chad said he would leave his cabinet more or less intact. Chad asked Jessica Gomez if she would be his Vice President and she was presently the Governor of Wyoming. Jessica accepted his offer and she became the Vice President. The first year went by uneventfully and his ratings as President were very high. The second year was also uneventful until he announced that he would not be seeking a second term. The party was good with that as Chad had gave the party a lot of dignity, and the belief that honesty prevailed. Chad recommended Jessica Gomez as the next presidential candidate that the National Party should endorse and support. The next two years were also uneventful except that Chad had a few health issues but the world as a whole was steady with some small skirmishes here and there but all in all it was serene. Arthur Sorenson again was running for President. As it turned out he was nominated by his party and Vice President Jessica Gomez was nominated as the choice for her party. Arthur was strong and he won the Presidency in a very close battle with Jessica. Jessica was young and she would return again. Chad did as he promised and just watched the two candidates and he formally retired at the end of his term and he handed the keys to his friend, President Arthur Sorenson. Chad predicted the Arthur Sorenson would be a great President. Chad had a stroke that sent him to the hospital. He was in and out of normal life and the doctors listed him in intensive care. As Chad laid there with wires monitoring all his vital signs he didn't know if he was delusional or not but Madeline appeared just as pretty as he remembered and she asked Chad if he would like to take the horses for a ride? Their two favorite horses were Prince and Princess and they were appaloosas a small breed of horse that the prairie Indians of America loved. They had a lot of endurance which the Indians liked because they traveled a lot.

The horse was their best friend. So, Chad asked the stable boy to saddle Prince and Princess and to make sure there were some apples and oats in the saddle bags. So, they took off like the wind. Suddenly the horses slowed to a walk and finally stopped. Chad and Madeline dismounted and peered over the chasm with the cold clear water flowing rapidly below. Madeline petted Princess and fed her a half of an apple. Prince was snuggling along Chad's body trying to find his treat. Finally, Chad relented and gave Prince his half an apple. Madeline let the reins fall and told Princess to go so the two horses went to a very verdant spot of green grass each blade swollen with moisture. Chad picked up Madeline and they started walking over the bridge.

Madeline was chattering like a magpie. Chad was kissing her face, eyes and lips with happy kisses from the tears streaming from both his eyes. Madeline said "Chad remember I said "curiosity killed the cat the first night we met?" Then I knelt down on the cold concrete sidewalk and petted your dog and I asked the little dog "What's your name?" and you said "Her name is Senior Crocker and her last name is Spaniel." We just met and we were already in love as you didn't remember answering the question, "What's your name?" We got to the other side of the chasm and a flock of white doves flew overhead and Madeline was gone, than I heard the lovely giggle and I knew that I would again hear it forever and I closed my eyes forever and just waited for Madeline to come to me.

The End.

www.ingramcontent.com/pod-product-compliance
Lightning Source LLC
LaVergne TN
LVHW061039070526
838201LV00073B/5108